Multicultural Folktales

for the Feltboard and Readers' Theater

by Judy Sierra

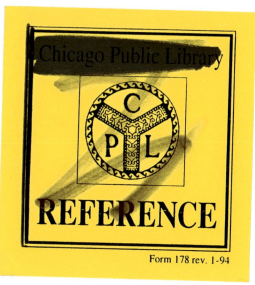

Oryx Press
1996

The rare Arabian oryx is believed to have inspired the myth of the unicorn. This desert antelope became virtually extinct in the early 1960s. At that time several groups of international conservationists arranged to have 9 animals sent to the Phoenix Zoo to be the nucleus of a captive breeding herd. Today the oryx population is over 1,000 and over 500 have been returned to the Middle East.

© 1996 by Oryx Press

4041 North Central at Indian School Road

Phoenix, Arizona 85012-3397

Published simultaneously in Canada

Printed and bound in the United States of America

∞ The paper used in this publication meets the minimum requirements of the American National Standard for Information Sciences—Permanence of Paper for Printed Library Materials, ANSI Z39.48-1984.

Library of Congress Cataloging-in-Publication Data

Sierra, Judy.
    Multicultural folktales for the feltboard and readers' theater/
by Judy Sierra.
        p. cm.
    Includes bibliographical references and index.
    ISBN 1-57356-003-0 (paper)
    1. Tales—Cross-cultural studies.   2. Tales—Study and teaching
(Elementary)   3. Storytelling.   4. Flannel boards.   5. Readers'
theater.   6. Teaching—Aids and devices.   I. Title.
GR69.S53   1996
398.2—DC20   96-35370
                                                                      CIP

CONTENTS

Preface v

Feltboard Storytelling and Readers' Theater 1

   Introduction to Feltboard Storytelling and Readers' Theater 3

Twenty Multicultural Folktales 11

  1   The New Year's Animals: A Chinese Folktale 13

  2   The Rabbit and the Tiger: A Vietnamese Folktale 24

  3   Kanchil and the Crocodile: An Indonesian Folktale 30

  4   Strongest of All: A Korean Folktale 38

  5   The Water Buffalo and the Snail: A Filipino Folktale 47

  6   The Bird and Her Babies: A Sri Lankan Folktale 54

  7   The Wolf, the Goat, and the Cabbages: An African Dilemma Tale 62

  8   Eat, Coat, Eat! A Turkish Folktale 68

  9   The Little Ant: A Spanish Folktale 76

  10 Munachar and Manachar: An Irish Folktale 85

  11 The Wee Bannock: A Scottish Folktale 97

  12 The Tricks of a Fox: A Folktale of the Koryak People of Siberia 107

  13 Through the Needle's Eye: An Inuit Folktale 116

  14 Brer Rabbit's Riding Horse: An African American Folktale 123

15 The Bad Bear: An Anglo-American Folktale 130

16 Juan and the Ghost: A Hispanic Folktale 138

17 The Rabbit Who Wanted Red Wings: An Anglo-American Folktale 146

18 The Mouse and the Coal: A French-Canadian Folktale 154

19 The Talkative Tortoise: A Guatemalan Folktale 163

20 The Two Monkeys: A Cuban Folktale 171

Bibliography 181

Index 185

PREFACE

good tale deserves to be told many times and in many different ways. This book was written for those who use stories, art, and drama in their work with children ages seven through twelve. It can be used by librarians, teachers, day-care providers, therapists, scout leaders, camp counselors, and parents. It is especially designed for busy people who don't have time to search for multicultural folktales, write their own plays, or design their own feltboard figures, yet who want high-quality material. In this book you will find twenty short, lively, tellable stories; elegantly simple patterns for feltboards; and readers' theater scripts that capture the essence of the characters and situations in language that is suitable for young readers.

I became fascinated with folktales nearly twenty years ago, when, as a new children's librarian, I discovered how tales from the oral tradition captivated child audiences—or should I say, how they enabled me to captivate child audiences. The folktale elicits the life experience of the teller so that each person ends up telling the same story a different way. I always loved the way folktales allowed me to embroider details onto them without losing track of the plot, how the characters just demanded my creative embellishment.

What were these bare skeletons of stories that sprang to life when I faced a group of children? Where did they come from? How had they stayed alive so long?

Such questions led me to long hours of research in university libraries and eventually to write a doctoral dissertation, "What Makes a Tale Tellable?" And after all these years, I've found that the most important thing to be said about folktales is, "Try one, tell one, they work."

Like my previous collections, this book consists of stories from as wide a range of cultures as possible, with special emphasis on ethnic groups in the United States. I have intentionally included lesser-known tales; however, experienced tellers will quickly note that these tales are similar to other, more familiar ones. The folktales in this book have been selected for their ability to cross cultures and to be readily understood and appreciated by contemporary elementary school children.

Each tale in the book is presented in two formats: in prose for storytelling and in script form for readers' theater. In a project that integrates reading, oral language, drama, and art, a leader could begin by reading or telling the folktale to a group of children. The group would then read the script, eventually presenting the play for an audience using readers' theater, either alone or with rod puppets.

Traceable patterns for feltboard figures are included with each tale. These patterns may also be enlarged and used to make flat paper rod puppets. Introductory chapters explain how to make a feltboard and feltboard figures as well as how to tell stories with the feltboard and through readers' theater.

As always, I owe a huge debt of gratitude to my husband Bob Kaminski, storyteller and producer extraordinaire of professional, school, and classroom theater. He drew the patterns for many of the feltboard figures in this book. Thanks also to Aaron Shepard for invaluable advice on creating readers' theater scripts.

Feltboard Storytelling and Readers' Theater

INTRODUCTION TO FELTBOARD STORYTELLING AND READERS' THEATER

Feltboard Storytelling

The stories in this book are perfect for telling in words alone, but there are many reasons for even the most accomplished storyteller to use the feltboard as well. Throughout the ages, storytellers have used visual artforms to enhance oral storytelling, from Inuit story knifing to Javanese story scrolls to Chinese shadow puppets. In western Australia, Aborigine storytellers would map their tales in the sand as they told them, using sticks and leaves to represent the story characters. For the contemporary storyteller, the feltboard is a way to engage a wider audience, including children who are not yet mature enough to sit and listen to a tale told only with words. This is particularly important to those who work with children they do not know well. A storyteller who can't anticipate a particular group's readiness to listen to stories is well-advised to have several feltboard stories in reserve. For teachers, the feltboard provides a different sort of benefit: children can use the feltboard figures to retell the stories they have heard, thus developing oral language skills.

In many storytellers' minds, feltboards are associated with unattractive, mass produced story figures. I believe that feltboard stories should be as attractive as the best children's books. They should be simple and bright, forming a pleasing composition on the feltboard. I design most feltboard figures in profile so that they appear to be interacting. Characters who speak to each other should be facing each other, for example. Some figures will have to be decorated on both sides so that they can face either left or right in the course of a story, and I indicate in the directions following each story which figures should be made double-sided.

If you aren't artistically inclined, seek out someone who is to make the figures for you. Artists who work in paint, crayon, or pastel can use these mediums on white interfacing—or fabric paints on felt. Fiber artists can create figures using machine quilting and fabric collage techniques.

Making a Feltboard

Feltboard made from an artist's portfolio

Feltboards may be purchased from school-supply companies, but they are simple to make. Despite its name, the feltboard is not covered with felt—felt is too fragile for the board, but is often used to make the figures. Rather, the board should be covered with non-stretch fabric that has a raised nap. The best fabrics are synthetics with a dull surface, such as robe velour. The best color for a feltboard is black, since dark colors will show less wear and tear. In addition, black will contrast beautifully with light, brightly colored feltboard figures.

To make a feltboard, cover a rectangle of stiff cardboard or lightweight wood with fabric, lapping and gluing about an inch of fabric over to the backside. A good size for a feltboard is 24 to 30 inches wide by 16 to 20 inches high. The board needs to rest at an angle so that the figures don't fall off. You can set it in the tray of an easel or chalkboard. A self-supporting feltboard can be made from a cardboard artist's portfolio. Cover one half of the inside with fabric and tie the side ties loosely to make the board sit on a tabletop.

Using the Patterns in This Book

The patterns which accompany the tales in this book are designed for a small feltboard, so feel free to enlarge them. When you do so, however, keep the same proportions; that is, enlarge each image by the same percentage. In deciding what size to make the figures, try not to think of the feltboard as a theater stage on which small figures will line up near the bottom edge. Rather, think of it as a movie screen that shows close-ups. Make your figures as large as they can be, without causing crowding when the maximum number of them appear together. Use the total space of the feltboard creatively: the lower and upper portions may represent the air and the ground in one story, foreground and background in another, a valley and a mountaintop in another.

Patterns can be traced directly onto white interfacing. If, however, you are making your figures from felt or similar fabric, you will need to photocopy the patterns, cut them out, then trace around them onto the cloth, using a fine-point marker.

Some of the figures need to be decorated on both sides, as noted in the instructions given with each story. In a few of these cases, the figures will be slightly different on each side. For example, the title character of "The Talkative Tortoise" must seem to have a smooth shell on one side and a cracked shell on the other. At the end of the story, the figure is turned over, showing how the tortoise's bad behavior gave him the cracked shell he has to this day.

Making Feltboard Figures

The figures used to tell a story on the feltboard are made from fabric or felt. These materials stick to the board by a combination of friction and static electricity. Some storytellers cut their feltboard figures from paper, which is made to stick to the feltboard by gluing pieces of felt, sandpaper, or Velcro to the back. I never recommend using paper for feltboard figures. White interfacing is inexpensive, takes paint and crayon as well as paper, and is much more durable. Moreover, paper figures cannot be made two-sided, which is required for many figures in this book, and paper figures cannot overlap each other.

There are several ways to make figures from fabric. Interfacing, which is sold at all fabric stores, is an ideal material. Interfacing comes in many varieties; ask for the white, nonwoven, nonfusible variety in medium or heavy weight. A yard will make three to four story sets. White interfacing is translucent, so you can trace the feltboard patterns directly onto it. Color the interfacing with crayons, artists' crayons, oil pastels, acrylic paint, or permanent markers, choosing colors that are light and bright so that they contrast strongly with the black feltboard (avoid navy blue and dark reds, greens, and browns). You will probably want to go over all the lines and features on each figure with a fine-point permanent black marker after you color them. Always color the figures before cutting them out.

Traditionally, feltboard figures have been made from felt. Felt figures have become much more jazzy and fun to make since the invention of fabric paints in squeezable tubes. These paints sit on the fabric surface in a raised line. They are available in many colors, including fluorescents, iridescents, and glitter-filled varieties, and are sold in fabric and craft stores. It takes a bit of practice to squeeze out a steady line of paint, but once you get the hang of it, decorating felt figures with fabric paints is easy. A reflective eye really makes a feltboard figure come alive, and the best way to achieve this is to glue on a sequin—a light-colored sequin on a dark background, or a dark one on a light one.

I often combine figures made of felt and interfacing in a single story set. It's easier, for example, to make people from interfacing, since the skin, hair, and costume tend to be different colors and textures. Multicolored figures such as these are faster and more effectively rendered with crayon or marker than with any other medium. It is faster, however, to make animals and other figures that are primarily one or two colors from felt, glue, and fabric paints.

Beautiful feltboard figures can be made using a collage of felt or other fabrics glued to a base of interfacing. To make these, first trace the figure twice: once onto paper and once onto interfacing, which will be the base for the collage. Cut the paper pattern into the appropriate pieces, then trace and cut these from felt or other fabric. Glue these pieces to the interfacing with white fabric glue. You can obtain an interesting stained-glass effect by using a background of *black* interfacing and cutting the collage pieces slightly smaller than the pattern pieces. This leaves an uneven and interesting black line between the colored pieces that make up the figure.

New arts-and-craft materials that may be used with the feltboard are constantly coming onto the market. For instance, sticky-backed felt is now available, making felt collage easier (if somewhat less permanent). Thin, brightly-colored foam sheets, available at craft stores, are useful for making scenery.

Creating Props and Scenery for the Feltboard

Tiny props are easy to lose, so always make duplicates, or even triplicates, to slide into your story folders. Some props are essential, such as the garbanzo bean in "The Two Monkeys." Others, such as the items the mouse trades in "The Mouse and the Coal," can be simply talked about and mimed, allowing listeners to picture them in their minds' eyes.

A feltboard story should be presented with a minimal amount of scenery—just enough to suggest locale. Too much scenery can detract from a story in two ways. First, it can visually overwhelm the figures, who should be the focus of the audience's attention. Second, placing and moving a lot of scenery can distract the storyteller from the thread of the story. Larger pieces of scenery are heavy and thus have a tendency to roll off the feltboard. It is a good idea to attach one or more small squares of Velcro to the backside of these. If scenery is to remain in place throughout the entire story, it can be attached to the fabric of the feltboard with pins.

I have not provided full-size patterns for generic scenery such as trees, tables, etc. Instead, I have included small sketches of these in a diagram of the entire feltboard found in the "Notes for Feltboard Storytelling" at the end of each folktale.

Rehearsing Feltboard Stories

I find that telling a story with the feltboard and placing and removing the figures are all part of one memory and performing process. I recommend waiting to learn a story until after you've made the figures and experimented with placing them on the board so that you can work any necessary pauses into the words of the tale. Once your figures are made, set up the feltboard and experiment with placing the figures as you read from the printed text, deciding when and where to position the characters. Placing the figures should be graceful, rhythmic, and carry much of the storytelling in and of itself. The position of the first figure or figures will determine how the feltboard looks as the storytelling progresses. Take time to decide how your story will unfold visually.

The storyteller's timing in revealing the figures can encourage or discourage audience participation. If you place a figure on the feltboard before you introduce it by name, children will automatically say or guess its name aloud. If you tell the audience the name of a figure before you place it, they will usually wait to see it in quiet anticipation.

Telling Feltboard Stories

Begin by setting up the board in a spot where all audience members will be able to see it. Any scenery or characters that need to be seen when the story begins should already be in place. The remaining figures should be in a pile in the order they will appear in the story. I like to set this stack of figures where the children can't see them but where I can easily reach them. I nearly always use a feltboard made from an artist's portfolio, and I hide the figures in the space on the tabletop between the front and back of the portfolio. Whenever possible, go through the process of arranging the figures just before you tell the story. That way, you won't be surprised in mid-story to find that a figure is missing. Also, placing the figures in order forces you to refresh the story's sequence of events in your mind.

If the audience has never seen a feltboard before, place a figure on the board and ask if anyone knows why it doesn't fall off. Unless you've used Velcro on your figures, there are two simple forces holding it in place: friction and static electricity. I explain friction by interlocking my fingertips and asking the children to imagine that my fingers are the little fibers sticking out from the cloth of the board and the figure. In order to explain static electricity, I ask if the children have noticed how their socks may stick to their sweaters when they come out of the clothes dryer. The force that keeps them together, of course, is static electricity.

It has been my experience that one telling is seldom enough for a feltboard story. If a group asks many content-related questions after a telling or asks to see the figures again, a retelling is probably in order. When there are repetitive chants and phrases, the children will enjoy joining in the second time a tale is told.

Children as Feltboard Storytellers

Young children delight in telling stories informally at the feltboard—to themselves or to each other—without any formal performer-audience arrangement. Older children, even first graders, can rehearse and tell stories for younger groups. Beginners can work in pairs, with one child telling the story and the other placing the figures, or they can each tell a part of the story. One or two children can work at the feltboard while others read the readers' theater script for that story.

Children in kindergarten and first grade enjoy creating small individual feltboards. These can be made from file folders with a rectangle of felt glued or stapled over half of the inside surface. The cloth for these individual feltboards does not need to be black, but may be any color. Figures can be made of interfacing, felt collage, or even paper with felt squares glued to the back to give a bit of friction. In classroom use, these individual feltboards are usually placed flat on a table or desk. The teacher tells the story while the children all practice putting the figures on their boards at the proper times. The feltboards can be sent home once the children know a story well enough to tell it on their own.

Bibliography

Sierra, Judy. *The Flannel Board Storytelling Book.* New York: H. W. Wilson, 1987.

———. *Mother Goose's Playhouse: Toddler Tales and Nursery Rhymes with Patterns for Puppets and Feltboards.* Ashland, OR: Bob Kaminski Media Arts, 1993.

Sierra, Judy, and Robert Kaminski. *Multicultural Folktales: Stories to Tell Young Children.* Phoenix: Oryx Press, 1991.

Readers' Theater

Readers' theater can be a simple classroom or library activity in which a group of children read a script aloud. Or, it can grow into a well-rehearsed staged performance for an audience, complete with costumes, sets, and props, in which each actor holds a script inconspicuously in one hand, referring to it when necessary. Group leaders should feel free to use and develop the practice of readers' theater and the scripts in this book to suit their own needs.

In general, feltboard storytelling is a way of presenting literature to pre-readers, and readers' theater is an activity for readers. Children over the age of eight often find feltboard stories too babyish; however, they will watch and listen with interest if they know that later they will have the opportunity to act out the story. Hearing the story first, even though the words of the script are different, primes the children's memory for plot and characters and facilitates guessing unknown words as they read the script.

Generally, the scripts in this book are for advanced third grade readers through sixth grade. "The Wee Bannock," "The Bad Bear," and "The Two Monkeys" are recommended for second and third grade readers, with the teacher taking the narrator role. Children will have to learn some new words, but they are used over and over. A little vocabulary goes a long way in a cumulative tale, giving the readers a great feeling of accomplishment. Which scripts you select for your group depends not only upon children's reading levels, but on the amount of time you can devote to preparing them for the projects and to rehearsal, both at home and in class.

Preparing the Scripts

To prepare the scripts in this book for use with your group, make a photocopy for each reader. Once roles have been assigned, highlighting pens can be used to mark all of one character's lines in each script. Scripts should be protected by a binder or folder of some sort.

You may want to adapt the script for your group. Common adaptations are splitting or combining the narrator roles, as described below, or changing the gender of characters to fit the gender of the reader. When a group of children will be performing a script, I always encourage them to make changes they think will make it better. The easiest changes to incorporate into a script are changes in the way things are said, and not plot changes.

First Readings

Expect first readings of a play to be rough. Readings will proceed much more smoothly, of course, if the readers know the story beforehand. You can summarize it for them, or read the story to them.

Caroline Bauer, in *Presenting Readers' Theater,* suggests a "round robin" initial script reading. The children sit in a circle, and unmarked scripts are distributed. Each child in turn reads one complete, uninterrupted speech of one character. This is a good way to try out a script to see if the group likes it and wants to proceed to an informal or formal performance. This also allows the leader to assess the children's reading and dramatic abilities, without any child feeling that a certain part belongs to him or her. After one or two readings participants can discuss the meaning and pronunciation of words and how to portray a character without any one reader feeling unduly criticized.

Narration

In readers' theater, a narrator, or group of narrators, sets the stage verbally for the audience and also describes many of the actions of the play. A teacher or other adult may take the role of narrator in a readers' theater production.

As is customary in readers' theater, the role of narrator is split among two or three readers in several of the scripts in this book. If need be, you can easily recombine these multiple narrators into one single part.

Readers' Theater for an Audience

The plays in this book can be developed and presented without any physical drama at all. Audiences of all ages enjoy listening to play readings, especially when the plays are short and easy to visualize, as the plays are in this book. The plays can even be recorded as a radio drama. Learning to deliver lines in character is enjoyable for children, especially since they have so many models to draw upon from film and television animation.

Readers' theater can also be moved to a stage, complete with costumes and props, entrances and exits, and action. If these performances are well-rehearsed, the audience will soon forget that the actors are reading from scripts.

A readers' theater play can also be illustrated with feltboard figures or with rod puppets. When using a feltboard, assign one or two students to place and remove the figures as the script is read. When using rod puppets, each reader can hold up a puppet as he reads his lines. The rod puppets can also move to a puppet stage. A cast of puppeteers can act out the story visually as another cast reads the script.

Flat paper rod puppets are quick and easy to make, using the patterns in this book enlarged to an appropriate size. These patterns are useful as well for reference when children design their own puppets. Rod puppets can be made from any relatively stiff paper such as construction paper or tagboard: the larger the puppet, the stiffer the paper must be. The paper is colored, painted, or decorated using collage, then attached to a rod made from a wood dowel, a piece of flat wood molding, or even a cardboard roll from paper towels or gift wrapping. A wooden or plastic ruler can be used as well. A staged puppet play will be more realistic if the puppets are decorated on both sides, which may entail making two puppets which are the mirror image of one another.

Bibliography

Bauer, Caroline Feller. *Presenting Reader's Theater*. New York: H. W. Wilson, 1991.

Laughlin, Mildred Knight, et. al. *Readers' Theater for Children: Scripts and Script Development*. Engelwood, CO: Libraries Unlimited, 1989.

———. *Social Studies Readers' Theater for Children: Scripts and Script Development*. Engelwood, CO: Libraries Unlimited, 1990.

Shepard, Aaron. *Stories on Stage: Scripts for Readers' Theater*. New York: H. W. Wilson, 1993.

Sierra, Judy. *Fantastic Theater: Puppets and Plays for Young Performers and Young Audiences*. New York: H. W. Wilson, 1991.

Sims, Judy. *Puppets for Dreaming and Scheming*. Walnut Creek, CA: Early Stages, 1976.

Sloyer, Shirlee. *Reader's Theatre: Story Dramatization for the Classroom*. Urbana, IL: NCTE, 1982.

Twenty Multicultural Folktales

THE NEW YEAR'S ANIMALS
A Chinese Folktale

This tale explains how the twelve animals of the zodiac were chosen and why the rat is the animal of the first year. Tales like this one are known in both China and Japan. Sometimes the ending was told differently: a race between the animals decided which would be first, or the rat won by cleverly hitching a ride on the ox's back.

It was long ago that the animals of the Chinese zodiac were chosen. In olden days, the creatures of forest and meadow had the power of speech. Great dragons could be seen rising from the mists of rivers. The Jade Emperor chose twelve animals, one to represent each year of the new calendar he had created.

He chose the rabbit because it was shy and graceful and the boar because it was brave and strong.

The high-spirited horse was one of the twelve, of course, and the shy, lovable sheep, too.

The dog—honest, fair, and faithful—could hardly be forgotten.

The dragon came next, in a blaze of color. Such a magnificent creature could never have been left out.

The emperor chose the monkey for its intelligence and friendliness.

The snake was selected for its wisdom as well as its lightning speed.

The ox came too, naturally, because it was a hard worker, patient and loyal.

The clever, scurrying rat followed the ox.

The tiger was one of the twelve because of its power and courage.

Last, but not least, came the colorful and energetic rooster.

"Now, let the cycle of years begin," proclaimed the Jade Emperor. "But which creature shall be first?" He looked at the twelve animals. "Which of you would be the beast of the first year?" he asked.

Now, most of the animals were content just to be one of the chosen twelve. Only the rat and the ox stepped forward.

"I deserve to be first," said the ox. "I have earned that right by being hardworking and faithful."

"I think I should be first," said the rat. "I am just as good in every way as the ox. And I am cleverer than he is."

The Jade Emperor found that he couldn't choose between the two. "Why don't we let the people decide which animal they like better," he said.

Hearing these words, the rat began to cry. "That isn't fair," he said. "I am so small that no one will see me. Of course they will choose the ox."

The Jade Emperor had magic powers, and he used them to make the rat bigger—three times bigger, in fact. "Now walk around a bit, and we'll see which one of you the people choose."

So the rat and the ox walked up and down the streets. Everywhere they went people said, "Just look at that rat!" and "I've never seen such a rat." No one even mentioned the ox. Why should they? They were used to seeing oxen exactly like him every day.

The Jade Emperor declared the rat to be the animal of the first year, recognizing that, once again, the rat had demonstrated his superior cleverness.

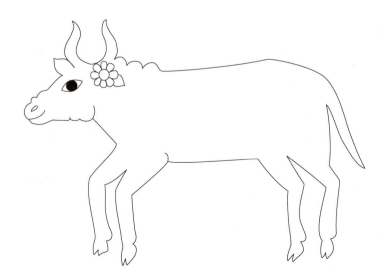

NOTES FOR FELTBOARD STORYTELLING

Make figures of the Jade Emperor, rabbit, boar, horse, sheep, dog, dragon, monkey, snake, ox, rat, bigger rat, tiger, and rooster. No scenery is necessary for this feltboard story. The patterns for these figures are more complicated than others in this book because they are based on traditional Chinese shadow puppet designs.

If you have trouble remembering the Emperor's reasons for choosing each animal, list the animals and their characteristics on a notecard and place it in your lap or on the table next to the feltboard.

When the rat and the ox begin to walk around town, encourage audience participation by telling the children, "Now, all of you can be the townspeople. When you see the rat that is three times bigger than any rat you've ever seen, what would you say?" Pause for improvised comments. "When you see the ox that looks just like every other ox you've ever seen, what would you say?" Pause again.

After telling the tale, arrange the animals, in order, in a circle on the feltboard and have the children name them. The following is the order of the animals, along with recent and future years they represent:

Rat 1984, 1996
Ox 1985, 1997
Tiger 1986, 1998
Rabbit 1987, 1999
Dragon 1988, 2000
Snake 1989, 2001
Horse.. 1990, 2002
Sheep 1991, 2003
Monkey 1992, 2004
Rooster 1993, 2005
Dog 1994, 2006
Boar 1995, 2007

Ox

Boar

Dragon

Sheep

Monkey

Big Rat

Horse

Rat

Rooster

Dog

Jade Emperor

Rabbit

Snake

Tiger

THE NEW YEAR'S ANIMALS
A Play for Readers' Theater

Thirteen characters plus townspeople and one narrator

Jade Emperor	Rabbit	Boar
Horse	Sheep	Dog
Dragon	Monkey	Snake
Ox	Rat	Tiger
Rooster		

NARRATOR: It was long ago that the animals of the Chinese zodiac were chosen. The Jade Emperor had created a new calendar, a cycle of twelve years. He decided to choose twelve animals, one for each of the years.

JADE EMPEROR: There. My list is finished. Will the twelve zodiac animals please step forward.

RABBIT: I am the rabbit, swift and graceful. I am pleased to be one of the twelve animals of the zodiac.

BOAR: I am the boar. I was chosen because I am so brave and strong. Of course I deserve to be one of the twelve animals.

HORSE: I am the horse, swift and high-spirited.

SHEEP: I am the sheep. I am not as strong or as beautiful as the horse, but I am shy and lovable.

DOG: It's me, the dog. I am honest, fair, and faithful. No group of animals would be complete without me.

DRAGON: I am the dragon. A magnificent creature like me could never have been left out.

MONKEY: It's me, the monkey. I am friendly and intelligent.

SNAKE: I am the snake. I was chosen for my great wisdom as well as my lightning speed.

OX: I am the ox. I am hard-working, patient, and loyal.

TIGER: I am the tiger. I was chosen for my power and courage.

RAT: I am the rat. What I lack in size, I make up for in cleverness.

ROOSTER: Without me, the rooster, how will the other animals know when New Year's Day begins?

JADE EMPEROR: Let the cycle of years begin!

RAT: But which creature shall be first?

JADE EMPEROR: Which one of you wants to be the beast of the first year?

NARRATOR: Now, most of the animals were content just to be one of the chosen twelve. Only the rat and the ox stepped forward.

OX: I deserve to be first. I have earned that right by being hard-working and faithful.

RAT: I think I should be first. Rats are survivors. We are tricky and clever. I am just as good as the ox in every way.

JADE EMPEROR: I cannot choose between you. Why don't we let the people decide.

RAT: (Crying) That's not fair! I am so small that no one will see me. Of course they will choose the ox.

NARRATOR: The Jade Emperor had magic powers in those days, and he used his magic to make the rat bigger, three times bigger, in fact.

JADE EMPEROR: Now walk around a bit, and we'll see which one of you the people like best.

NARRATOR: So the rat and the ox walked up and down the streets.

TOWNSPEOPLE: Just look at that rat! What a huge rat! Who has ever seen such a big rat?

JADE EMPEROR: And what do you think of the ox?

TOWNSPEOPLE: What ox? Oh, him. He is just . . . well . . . ordinary.

OX: I think the rat tricked me.

JADE EMPEROR: The rat shall be the animal of the first year, for once again, he has demonstrated his superior cleverness.

THE RABBIT AND
THE TIGER
A Vietnamese Folktale

For the people who live in its domain, the tiger has always been a frightening beast, and with good reason. Yet in many of the folktales from Asia, the tiger is a dupe—a character who is easy to fool and who never learns from past mistakes. Perhaps these tales helped ease people's fears of the mighty creature. The tiger in this tale from Vietnam is a perfect example of a dupe.

There once was a tiger—a very large, very hungry tiger—and he thought the other animals in the jungle had been put there simply to satisfy his appetite. The smaller animals lived in fear of him, and the tiger always got his way. But a rabbit, who was known for her tricks, decided to teach the tiger a lesson: brains can overcome brute force.

The first time that the tiger met the rabbit, the rabbit was nibbling some vegetables in a farmer's garden.

"Grrrrr!" growled the tiger. "It's my lunch time, and I am hungry!"

The rabbit looked around. She saw a chili plant nearby. "It wouldn't be a good idea for you to eat me," she told the tiger. "Do you see the red fruits on that bush over there?" the rabbit asked. She pointed her paw toward the chilies.

The tiger had never paid much attention to chilies, since he didn't eat vegetables. He looked at the chilies. "Yes," he yawned. "I see them."

"Those tasty little fruits are the source of the king's power, and I am guarding them for him. It wouldn't be good for anyone else to get that power, would it?"

The tiger said to himself, "I am going to eat those sweet fruits, and then I will be as powerful as the king." He began tearing the chilies off the bush with his teeth and chewing them. The rabbit backed slowly into the trees, then turned and hopped away. She wasn't around when the chilies began to burn the tiger's insides.

"The king's stomach must be more powerful than mine," said the tiger to himself. He roared in pain and raced off into the jungle.

The next time the tiger saw that rabbit, the rabbit was resting beside a tree. "This time I will eat you before you trick me," he growled.

The rabbit looked all around, and by chance she spied a wasps' nest hanging from the branch of a tree. "The king will be very angry if you eat me," said the rabbit, "because I am guarding his drum. I must make sure that no one but the king plays this drum. It is too good for anyone but him."

"Hah!" said the tiger to himself. "I can play the king's drum if I want to." Then he turned to the rabbit and growled, "Get away from here, right now!"

And so the rabbit hopped off. The tiger reached up and hit the king's drum—*thump, thump*—with his paw. *Bzzzzzz! Bzzzzzz!* Was he ever sorry!

The next time the tiger found the rabbit, the tiger's body was still aching and swollen from all the bites those wasps had given him. "Rabbit!" cried the tiger. "Prepare to be my dinner!"

The rabbit looked up. She saw a snake slowly sliding down a tree trunk. "I would gladly be your dinner," the rabbit told the tiger, "but can't you see that I am busy now? I am taking the king's belt to him." She pointed to the snake. "When the king wears this belt, no power in the world can overcome him."

"Then it should be MY belt," the tiger roared. He took the cobra in his paws and wrapped it around his middle. "It's my belt now, " he said. But the rabbit didn't hear him. She was long gone, and she hasn't seen the tiger since.

NOTES FOR FELTBOARD STORYTELLING

Make figures of the tiger, the rabbit, and the snake, using the included patterns. The swarm of wasps should be represented by a buzzing sound. Children will see the wasps in their minds' eyes as you make this noise. Make a chile bush, tree, and wasp nest to fit your feltboard, based on the figure on the following page.

This story has three different scenes. At the end of each of the first two scenes, remove all the figures from the feltboard, then set it up for the next scene. The audience will enjoy guessing, based on the new additions, how the rabbit will trick the tiger *this* time.

Rabbit

Snake

Tiger

27

THE RABBIT AND THE TIGER
A Play for Readers' Theater

Six or more characters and one narrator

Rabbit	**Snake**
Tiger	**Wasps (3 or more)**

NARRATOR: There once was a tiger—a very large, very hungry tiger—and he thought the other animals in the jungle had been put there simply to satisfy his appetite. The smaller animals lived in fear of him, and the tiger always got his way. But a rabbit, who was known for her tricks, decided to teach the tiger a lesson—that brains can overcome brute force.

TIGER: Grrrr! It's my lunch time, and I am HUNGRY.

NARRATOR: The rabbit looked around and saw a chili plant nearby. Quickly, she thought of a plan.

RABBIT: It wouldn't be a good idea for you to eat me now. Do you see the fruits on that bush over there?

TIGER: Yes, I see them.

RABBIT: Those fruits are the source of the king's power, and I am guarding them. It wouldn't be right for anyone else to get that power, would it?

TIGER: I am going to eat those sweet fruits. Then I will be as powerful as the king.

NARRATOR: The rabbit backed quietly into the trees, and then she ran away. So she wasn't around when the chilies began to burn the tiger's insides.

TIGER: Rarrrrr! Ow! Ow-o-o-o-o! The king's stomach must be stronger than mine.

NARRATOR: The next time the tiger found that rabbit, she was resting beside a tree.

TIGER: Rabbit, this time I will eat you before you trick me.

NARRATOR: The rabbit quickly looked around. She saw a wasps' nest hanging from a branch of the tree.

RABBIT: The king would be angry if you did, because right now, this very instant, I am guarding his drum. Do you see it up there, hanging from that branch? I must make sure that no one but the king plays this drum. It is too good for anyone but him.

TIGER: Hah! I can play the king's drum if I want to. Grrrr! Get away from here, right now!

NARRATOR: And so the rabbit hopped away. She knew what the tiger would do. He would grab the wasps' nest and hit it—*thump, thump*—with his paw. But she was long gone when he did.

WASPS: Bzzzzzzz.

TIGER: Ow! Owoooooo!

WASPS: Bzzzzzzz.

NARRATOR: The next time the tiger found that rabbit, the tiger was really mad. His body was still aching from all those wasp bites.

TIGER: Grrrr! There you are, you tricky rabbit. Prepare to be my dinner!

NARRATOR: The rabbit looked up. She saw a snake slowly sliding down the tree trunk.

SNAKE: Sssssssss.

RABBIT: Can't you see that I am busy? I am taking the king's belt to him. He left it wrapped around this tree. When the king wears this belt, no one in the world can overcome him.

TIGER: Then it should be MY belt!

NARRATOR: The tiger took the cobra in his paws and wrapped it around his middle.

SNAKE: Sssssssss.

TIGER: It's my belt now

SNAKE: Chomp.

TIGER: Ow! Ow-o-o-o!

NARRATOR: But the rabbit was too far away to hear him, and she never saw the tiger again.

3

KANCHIL AND THE CROCODILE
An Indonesian Folktale

Kanchil is the Indonesian name for the mouse deer—a small animal that looks like a deer but is only about two feet tall. The mouse deer has small tusks in its mouth and no horns on its head. In the folktales of Indonesia, Kanchil is a tricky character, always outsmarting stronger animals like the tiger and the crocodile.

Once upon a time, a crocodile was basking in the sun on the bank of a river, when, suddenly, a tree fell on top of him. The crocodile tried to crawl out from under the tree, but it was too heavy. He couldn't move. He was trapped. He called out for someone to help him.

Along came a water buffalo. Now, the water buffalo was a good creature. He was helpful and strong. But he wasn't a fast thinker. Just what the crocodile was looking for.

"Oh, dear friend," said the crocodile in his nicest voice, "please have pity on me. Use your hard horns and your strong shoulders to push this tree off my back."

30

The water buffalo said he would try. Though he pushed with all his might, the tree wouldn't budge. Its roots were holding it in place. So the patient water buffalo chewed through the roots and then was able to roll the tree off the crocodile's back.

The water buffalo waited for the crocodile to thank him, but the crocodile only moaned more pitifully than before. "Oh, my aching bones. I can't move. Would you mind pushing me back into the river?"

The water buffalo nudged the crocodile to the water's edge. But the crocodile still wasn't happy. He knew he could not grab the water buffalo and hold him tight until he was in deep water.

"My legs are so sore that I can't swim," he said. "Please push me out into the deep water."

The water buffalo pushed the crocodile into the deep water. The crocodile then turned, opened his mouth, and locked his jaws on the water buffalo's neck.

"What are you doing?" cried the water buffalo.

"I am getting ready to eat you," answered the crocodile. "You were foolish enough to come into the water with a crocodile, and so you deserve to be eaten."

"But I saved your life!" the water buffalo sputtered. "You should be grateful to me. Let me go!"

Just then, an old basket floated up to them.

"The crocodile is right," said the basket. "Look at me! I served a family for years. I carried things to the market for them. But when I got a bit old, they threw me into the river. No one is grateful. You, water buffalo, should have known better. Go ahead and eat him, crocodile."

"You see?" said the crocodile. "I am right."

"Let's ask someone else," the water buffalo pleaded. "If two more creatures agree with you, you can eat me. But if either of the two agrees with me, you must let me go."

The crocodile went along with the water buffalo's plan. Soon, a rice bowl floated by. It was cracked in the middle. The crocodile explained to the rice bowl what had happened and asked for its opinion.

"Why should you be grateful?" said the rice bowl to the crocodile. "Is anyone grateful? I served rice to people for years. Then, when I became cracked, they threw me into the river, even though I am still good for something. Go ahead, crocodile. Eat him."

The crocodile licked his lips, and the water buffalo moaned sadly. Then they heard a tiny voice. It came from the riverbank. It was Kanchil, the tricky mouse deer.

"What seems to be the matter?" Kanchil asked them.

"Kanchil, friend," said the crocodile. "Please help us decide something. I was sunning myself on the riverbank when . . . .

"What?" Kanchil interrupted. "Where were you sunning yourself?"

"On the riverbank," the crocodile told him.

31

"Which riverbank?" Kanchil asked.

"The one where you are standing," the crocodile answered, "only a little bit farther on, by that fallen tree."

"Would you mind showing me exactly?" Kanchil asked him.

The crocodile let go of the water buffalo and swam to the river bank. He crawled out next to the fallen tree.

"Here," he said. "And this tree was on top of me."

Kanchil laughed. "I don't believe that tree was on top of you."

"It was," grunted the crocodile. "Come here, water buffalo, and roll it on top of me, just like it was before."

The water buffalo came onto the river bank and rolled the tree on top of the crocodile.

"Now I understand," laughed Kanchil. "I hope that both of you understand, too."

But the water buffalo didn't hear him. He had already run off through the trees and was far, far away.

NOTES FOR FELTBOARD STORYTELLING

Make figures of the crocodile, water buffalo, Kanchil, rice bowl, and basket. Cut along the mouth line of the crocodile. Separate the crocodile's mouth and place the water buffalo's neck between his jaws at the appropriate point in the story. Make the tree that falls on the crocodile and a few bushes, as shown in the figure below. Cut and decorate a piece of blue felt or foam to represent the river. Conceal Kanchil behind (under) a bush, revealing him when the story requires.

Water Buffalo

Rice Bowl

Basket

Kanchil

Crocodile

KANCHIL AND THE CROCODILE
A Play for Readers' Theater

Five characters and one narrator

Crocodile   **Rice Bowl**

Water Buffalo   **Kanchil**

Basket

NARRATOR: Once, a crocodile was basking in the sun on the bank of a river, when a tree fell on top of him. He tried to crawl out from under the tree, but it was too heavy. He was trapped.

CROCODILE: Oh, boo hoo! Oh, boo hoo! Won't someone please come and save me?

NARRATOR: Along came a water buffalo. He was helpful, and he was strong. But he wasn't a fast thinker. Just what the crocodile was looking for.

CROCODILE: Oh, dear friend, please have pity on me. Use your hard horns and your strong shoulders to push this tree off my back.

WATER BUFFALO: I'll try.

NARRATOR: The water buffalo put his head to the tree and pushed with all his might, but the tree wouldn't budge.

CROCODILE: The tree's roots are holding it. Bite through the roots, won't you please?

WATER BUFFALO: Very well.

NARRATOR: So the water buffalo patiently chewed through all the tree's roots, and then he was able to roll the tree off the crocodile. He waited for the crocodile to thank him.

CROCODILE: Oh, my aching bones. I can't move. Would you mind pushing me back into the river?

WATER BUFFALO: No, I don't mind.

NARRATOR: The water buffalo nudged the crocodile to the water's edge. But the crocodile still wasn't happy. He knew he could not grab the water buffalo and hold him tight until he was in deep water.

35

CROCODILE: Oh, my legs are so sore that I can't swim. Push me out into the deep water.

NARRATOR: The water buffalo pushed the crocodile into the deep water. The crocodile then turned, opened his mouth, and locked his jaws on the water buffalo's neck.

WATER BUFFALO: What are you doing?

CROCODILE: I am getting ready to eat you. You were foolish enough to come into the water with a crocodile, and so you deserve to be eaten.

WATER BUFFALO: I saved your life! You should be grateful to me. Let me go!

CROCODILE: Crocodiles are not grateful. Crocodiles are hungry.

WATER BUFFALO: You can't do this. It isn't right.

NARRATOR: Just then, an old basket floated up to them.

BASKET: The crocodile is right, you know. Look at me! I served a family for years. I carried things to the market for them. But when I got a bit old, they threw me into the river. No one is grateful. You, water buffalo, should have known better. Go ahead and eat him, crocodile.

CROCODILE: You see? I am right.

WATER BUFFALO: Let's ask someone else. If two more creatures agree with you, you can eat me. But if either of the two agrees with me, you must let me go.

CROCODILE: Very well. It's a deal.

NARRATOR: A rice bowl floated by. It was cracked in the middle.

CROCODILE: Hey, rice bowl! Give us your advice. A tree fell on me and this water buffalo rolled it off me.

WATER BUFFALO: I saved his life.

CROCODILE: Then he was foolish enough to push me into the deep water. This silly water buffalo thinks I should be grateful and let him go.

RICE BOWL: Why should you be grateful? Is anyone grateful? I served rice to people for years. Then, when I became cracked, they threw me into the river, even though I am still good for something. Go ahead, crocodile, eat him.

CROCODILE: Heh, heh, heh. Supper time.

WATER BUFFALO: (Sadly) Ooooooh.

NARRATOR: Then a tiny voice came from the riverbank. It was Kanchil, the tricky mouse deer.

KANCHIL: What seems to be the problem?

CROCODILE: Kanchil, friend, please help us decide something. I was sunning myself on the riverbank when . . . .

KANCHIL: (Interrupting) Where were you sunning yourself?

CROCODILE: On the riverbank.

KANCHIL: Which riverbank?

CROCODILE: The one where you are standing, only a little bit farther on, by that fallen tree.

KANCHIL: Would you mind showing me exactly where?

NARRATOR: The crocodile let go of the water buffalo and swam to the river bank. He crawled out next to the fallen tree.

CROCODILE: Here. And this tree was on top of me.

KANCHIL: (Laughing) I don't believe that tree was on top of you.

CROCODILE: It was. Come here, water buffalo, and roll it on top of me, just like it was before.

WATER BUFFALO: Gladly. Umph! Umph! There, Kanchil, that is exactly how it was.

KANCHIL: Now I understand. I hope that both of you understand, too.

NARRATOR: But the water buffalo didn't hear him. He was already running off through the trees and was far, far away.

STRONGEST OF ALL
A Korean Folktale

This is a circular tale, a kind of tale that is widely known in India and other parts of Asia. In these tales, there is a search for the strongest, most powerful creature or force of nature in the world, and the search nearly always leads right back to the seeker. Circular tales repeat the same scene several times with minor variations, so they are easy for children to both follow as an audience and learn to tell themselves. In this Korean folktale, a mother and father mole search for the most powerful creature as a husband for their daughter.

In Korea there are many tall stone statues, which are called *miryuk.* This is the story of a family of moles that lived in a tunnel under one of these statues. There was a mother mole, a father mole, and their beloved daughter mole. Like all parents, the mother mole and father mole thought that their daughter was the most wonderful child ever born. So when a young-man mole who lived in the tunnel next door came to see them, asking to marry their daughter, the father and mother moles answered, "No, no! Our daughter will never marry a common mole." And the young mole went sadly home.

Now their daughter, who liked the mole next door very much, asked, "If I can't marry a mole, who can I marry?"

Her parents thought for a while and finally said, "You can only marry the strongest of all creatures."

"Who is that?" asked the daughter.

"You must marry the sun," her father replied. "The sun lights all of the earth. The sun is the strongest of all."

So the father mole left home and walked a long way until, at last, he came to the top of a mountain. He looked up at the sun and said, "Great Sun. I have a daughter who is the prettiest, smartest, nicest mole in the world. She can only marry the strongest of all. Would you marry my daughter?"

But the sun replied, "I cannot, for I am not the strongest of all. There is someone stronger who covers me up and blocks my light. Your daughter should marry the cloud."

"Yes! Of course. The cloud," said the father mole, and he thanked the sun for his advice. He decided to search for the cloud, but he didn't have to travel far, for soon a big dark cloud moved across the sky and covered the sun.

"Great Cloud," said the father mole, "I have a daughter who is the smartest, nicest, prettiest mole in the world. She can only marry the strongest of all. And that must be you, because you cover the sun. Will you marry my daughter?"

But the cloud replied, "I am sorry, but I am so weak that the wind can blow me right out the sky. Look out! Here comes the wind now."

Sure enough, a great gust of wind hit the mountaintop. It swept the cloud out of sight and lifted the father mole up into the air, setting him down right next to the stone statue.

"Stop! Wind, listen to me!" cried the father mole. "I have a daughter who is the smartest, nicest, prettiest mole on earth. She can only marry the strongest of all. And that must be you, because you blew the cloud out of the sky. Will you marry my daughter?"

But the wind replied, "No-o-o, I can't do that. I am not the strongest of all. Look! This stone statue stops me still. Your daughter should marry the stone statue."

The wind changed direction and was gone. The mole gazed up at the face of the stone statue. "Powerful stone statue," he said, "I have a daughter. You must have seen her. She lives right under your feet. She is the nicest, prettiest, smartest mole on earth, and she must marry the strongest of all. That must be you because you stop the wind. Will you marry my daughter?"

But the stone statue replied, "If you think that I am the strongest of all, you are wrong. Right now a tiny animal is digging under my feet. He will make me fall down in ruins some day. That animal is a mole."

The father mole turned and saw dirt flying from the entrance of a nearby tunnel. A small, hard-working mole poked his nose out. It was the same mole that had asked to marry his daughter. Now the father mole had to be very, very polite.

"Excuse me," he said. "Will you please marry my daughter? She can only marry the strongest of all. That must be you because you have the power to bring down the stone statue. Will you marry her?"

The mole next door agreed. Now everyone was happy, especially the moles' daughter, for he was the husband she wanted all along.

NOTES FOR FELTBOARD STORYTELLING

Make figures of the father mole, mother mole, daughter mole, mole next door, sun, cloud, wind, and statue. The designs for the sun, cloud, and wind are based on masked characters from Korean folk drama. The clothing of the moles is traditional, except that of the mole next door who is a modern young mole, in a t-shirt and sunglasses. The stone statue should remain on the feltboard during the entire story. You needn't make scenery to represent the mountain that the father mole climbs; designate one of the upper corners of the feltboard as this locale, and the children will see it in their imaginations.

Wind

Cloud

Mother

Sun

Daughter

Father

Mole Next Door

Great Stone Statue

STRONGEST OF ALL
A Play for Readers' Theater

Eight characters and one narrator

Father Mole	**Mole Next Door**	**Wind**
Mother Mole	**Sun**	**Stone Statue**
Daughter Mole	**Cloud**	

NARRATOR: In Korea there are many tall stone statues, which are called *miryuk*. This is the story of a family of moles that lived in a tunnel under one of these statues. There was a mother mole, a father mole, and a daughter mole. Like all parents, the mother mole and father mole thought that their daughter was the most wonderful child ever born.

MOTHER MOLE: Isn't she precious.

FATHER MOLE: Isn't she clever.

DAUGHTER MOLE: Mom! Dad! Stop it!

NARRATOR: One morning, the young-man mole who lived in the tunnel next door came to see them.

MOLE NEXT DOOR: I would like to marry your daughter.

FATHER MOLE: No!

MOTHER MOLE: No!

FATHER MOLE AND MOTHER MOLE: Never!

DAUGHTER MOLE: I like him.

FATHER MOLE: You can't marry a lowly mole who lives in a dirty tunnel in the earth.

DAUGHTER MOLE: But we live in a dirty tunnel in the earth.

MOTHER MOLE: Hush!

NARRATOR: And so the mole next door went sadly home.

DAUGHTER MOLE: If I can't marry a mole, who *can* I marry?

MOTHER MOLE: You may only marry the strongest of all.

FATHER MOLE: You must marry the sun, for the sun lights all of the earth. The sun is the strongest of all.

MOTHER MOLE: Hurry! Go ask the sun to marry her.

NARRATOR: So the father mole left home and walked a long way. At last he came to the top of a mountain. He looked up at the sun.

FATHER MOLE: Great sun! I have a daughter who is the prettiest, smartest, nicest mole in the world. She can only marry the strongest of all, and that must be you. Would you marry my daughter?

SUN: It is kind of you to ask, but I am not the strongest of all. There is someone stronger who covers me up and blocks my light. Your daughter should marry the cloud.

FATHER MOLE: Yes! Of course. The cloud. Thank you.

NARRATOR: So the mole began to search for the cloud. He didn't have to go far. Soon big dark cloud moved across the sky and covered the sun.

FATHER MOLE: Great cloud! I have a daughter who is the smartest, nicest, prettiest mole in the world. She can only marry the strongest of all, and that must be you because you cover the sun. Will you marry my daughter?

CLOUD: I am sorry, but I am so weak that the wind can blow me right out of the sky. Look out! Here comes the wind right now.

NARRATOR: Sure enough, a strong wind hit the mountaintop. It swept the cloud out of sight and lifted the father mole up in the air, setting him down right next to the stone statue.

FATHER MOLE: Wind! Stop! Listen to me! I have a daughter who is the smartest, nicest, prettiest mole in the world. She can only marry the strongest of all, and that must be you because you blew the cloud out of the sky. Will you marry my daughter?

WIND: No-o-o, I can't do that. I am not the strongest of all. Look! This stone statue stops me still. Your daughter should marry the stone statue.

NARRATOR: In an instant, the wind was gone. The mole looked up at the face of the stone statue.

FATHER MOLE: Powerful stone statue, I have a daughter. You must have seen her. She lives right under your feet. She is the nicest, prettiest, smartest mole in the world. She must marry the strongest of all, and that must be you because you stop the wind. Will you marry my daughter?

STONE STATUE: If you think that I am the strongest of all, you are wrong. Right now a tiny animal is digging under my feet. One day, he will make me fall down. That animal is a mole.

NARRATOR: The father mole saw dirt flying out of a nearby tunnel. A small mole poked his nose out. It was the same mole that wanted to marry his daughter.

FATHER MOLE: (Very politely) Excuse me. Will you please marry my daughter? She can only marry the strongest of all, and that must be you because you have the power to bring down the stone statue. Will you marry her?

MOLE NEXT DOOR: Yes!

DAUGHTER MOLE: Finally.

MOTHER MOLE: Who would have guessed that the mole next door was strongest of all!

THE WATER BUFFALO AND THE SNAIL
A Filipino Folktale

Tales of the race between the very swift animal and the extremely slow animal are found in nearly every one of the world's cultures. In this tale from the Philippines, the water buffalo doesn't really lose the race, but he *thinks* he has lost, which is just as bad. This happens because he is not observant enough to tell one tiny snail from another.

Once, a water buffalo went to a well to get a drink of water. On the edge of the well he saw a snail moving along very, very slowly. The water buffalo was fascinated, and he watched the snail for a long time.

At last the snail asked, "Why are you staring at me?"

"I can't believe that any creature could move as slowly as you," replied the water buffalo.

"I am not slow," sniffed the snail. "Why, I could easily beat you in a race."

This made the water buffalo laugh. "Shall we race to that tree over there?" he asked.

"No, no, no," said the snail. "I can only beat you in a long race all around the island. Meet me here in three days and then we'll race."

So the water buffalo agreed. Meanwhile, the snail sent out word to all her friends and relations that the race would take place in three days. She told them that whenever they saw the water buffalo, they should say:

Hello, water buffalo.
Why are you so slow?

Now, there were so many snails on that island that none of them had to travel far in order for all of them to learn about the plan.

The day of the race came, and the water buffalo returned to the well where he had met the snail.

"Are you ready?" he asked the snail.

"Yes," the snail answered.

The water buffalo raced northward along the coast, but soon he grew thirsty. He stopped at another well to drink. As he was bending his head down, he heard a tiny voice:

Hello, water buffalo.
Why are you so slow?

The water buffalo looked around and saw a tiny, familiar shape. He thought it was the same snail he had seen at the first well. But, of course, it wasn't. The water buffalo was now afraid of losing the race, and he began to run, without even stopping to drink. He ran and ran until he was so thirsty he paused at a freshwater pool. As he drank, he heard a little laugh:

Tee, hee, hee, hee, hee.
Hello, water buffalo.
Why are you so slow?

"Oh no!" cried the water buffalo. "Are you here already?

The water buffalo sped onward, even faster than before, but he soon grew weary. He could barely stumble back to the well where the race had begun. "Please don't let the snail be here," he muttered. But there sat the snail, and the snail was singing.

Hello, water buffalo.
Why are you so slow?

The water buffalo was so angry, he stamped his hooves against a stone. His hooves split.

The hooves of the water buffalo are split today because that one water buffalo, long ago, thought that a snail had beaten him in a race. Since then, whenever a group of snails get together, they remember how they tricked the mighty water buffalo, and they all laugh, "Tee, hee, hee, hee, hee."

NOTES FOR FELTBOARD STORYTELLING

Make the figure of the water buffalo two-sided. One side, which faces the snails, has hooves without lines on them. On the reverse side, lines on the hooves indicate that they are split. The snails are part of the scenery—they sit atop two wells and a pool. The water buffalo encounters the first snail at the bottom center of the board, the second at the top right, and the third at the top left. At the end of the story, turn the water buffalo over to show his split hooves.

Water Buffalo

Show these lines on one
side only

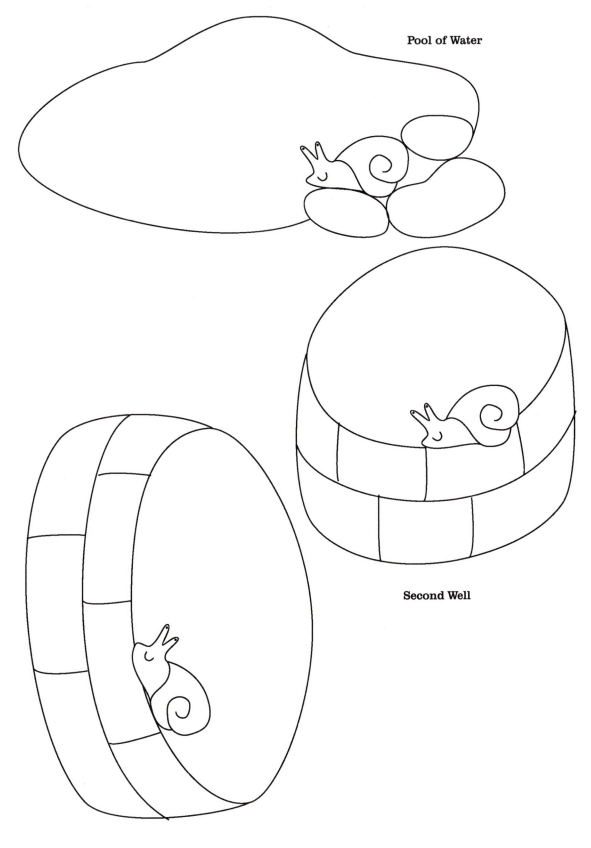

Pool of Water

Second Well

First Well

THE WATER BUFFALO AND THE SNAIL
A Play for Readers' Theater

Four characters and two narrators

Water Buffalo   **Snail 2**

Snail 1   **Snail 3**

NARRATOR 1: Once, a water buffalo went to a well to get a drink of water.

NARRATOR 2: On the edge of the well he saw a snail moving very, very slowly. The water buffalo watched the snail for a long time.

SNAIL 1: Why are you looking at me?

WATER BUFFALO: I can't believe that any animal could move as slowly as you do.

SNAIL 1: I am not slow. If I wanted to, I could beat you in a race.

WATER BUFFALO: Ha! Ha! Shall we race to that tree over there?

SNAIL 1: No, I can only beat you in a long race all around the island. Meet me here in three days, and then we'll race.

WATER BUFFALO: All right, I will.

NARRATOR 1: The snail sent word to all her friends and relations that a race would take place in three days.

NARRATOR 2: She told them that whenever they saw the water buffalo, they should say:

SNAIL 1: Hello, water buffalo.
Why are you so slow?

NARRATOR 1: Soon every snail on the island knew of the plan.

NARRATOR 2: The day of the race came: The water buffalo returned to the well where he had met the snail.

WATER BUFFALO: Snail, are you ready?

SNAIL 1: Yes, I am. On your mark, get set, go!

NARRATOR 1: The water buffalo raced northward along the coast. But soon he grew thirsty and stopped at another well to drink. As he was bending his head down, he heard a tiny voice.

Snail 2: Hello, water buffalo.
Why are you so slow?

Water Buffalo: How did you get here so fast?

Narrator 1: The water buffalo thought it was the same snail he had seen at the first well. But of course, it wasn't. He was afraid he would lose the race.

Narrator 2: He ran and ran until he was so thirsty he had to stop at a freshwater pool. He lapped up the water, and as he did so, he heard a little laugh.

Snail 3: Tee, hee, hee, hee, hee!
Hello, water buffalo.
Why are you so slow?

Water Buffalo: Oh no! Are you here already, my little friend?

Narrator 1: The water buffalo ran on even faster than before, but he soon tired himself out.

Narrator 2: He could barely stagger back to the well where the race had begun.

Water Buffalo: (To himself) Please don't let the snail be here.

Narrator 1: But there sat the snail. The snail was singing:

Snail 1: Hello, water buffalo,
Why are you so slow?

Narrator 1: The water buffalo was so angry that he stamped his hooves against a stone. His hooves split. They are still split today, all because he thought that a snail had beaten him in a race.

Narrator 2: And whenever the snails get together, they talk about the trick they played on the mighty water buffalo, and they all laugh.

Snails 1, 2, and 3: Tee, hee, hee, hee, hee!

THE BIRD AND HER BABIES
A Sri Lankan Folktale

hain tales like this one exist in the folklore of many countries. Two examples are the Irish folktale, "Munachar and Manachar," and the Cuban folktale, "The Two Monkeys," both in this book. A chain tale features a character who needs to get something done and who asks a series of people, animals, and even objects to help. All but the last one refuse. In the course of the tale, however, a highly effective chain reaction is set up that unwinds once someone agrees to help.

A bird pecked a hole in the trunk of a hollow tree and built a nest inside. She laid her eggs, and when they hatched, the baby birds were hungry. The mother bird fed them well, morning, noon, and night. The babies grew fat. When it was time for them to leave the nest and learn to fly, they were too large to get out of the hole in the tree.

So the mother bird went to the carpenter and asked him to cut the hole bigger so that her babies could get out and learn to fly. But the carpenter said, "No, why should I?"

Then the bird went to a snake and asked the snake to bite the carpenter, because the carpenter wouldn't cut the tree, and the bird's babies couldn't get out and learn to fly. But the snake said, "No, why should I?"

Then the bird went to the elephant, and asked the elephant to step on the snake, because the snake wouldn't bite the carpenter, and the carpenter wouldn't cut the tree, and the bird's babies couldn't get out and learn to fly. But the elephant said, "No, why should I?"

Then the bird met a mouse. She asked the mouse to get inside the elephant's trunk and tickle him, because the elephant wouldn't step on the snake, and the snake wouldn't bite the carpenter, and the carpenter wouldn't cut the tree, and the bird's babies couldn't get out and learn to fly. But the mouse said, "No, why should I?"

Then the bird found a cat. She asked the cat to chase the mouse, because the mouse wouldn't tickle the elephant, and the elephant wouldn't step on the snake, and the snake wouldn't bite the carpenter, and the carpenter wouldn't cut the tree, and the bird's babies couldn't get out and learn to fly.

And the cat said "Why shouldn't I chase the mouse? It would be my pleasure."

Then the cat began to chase the mouse, the mouse began to tickle the elephant's trunk, the elephant began to step on the snake, the snake began to bite the carpenter, the carpenter cut open the tree, and the bird's babies got out and learned to fly. And that's the end!

NOTES FOR FELTBOARD STORYTELLING

Make figures of the mother bird, three baby birds, the carpenter, the snake, the elephant, the mouse, and the cat. In addition, make a tree of felt or similar opaque material; it must be large enough to cover the baby birds, revealing only their heads and beaks. Before the children see the feltboard, hide the babies underneath the tree so that they can't be seen. Place the mother to the left of the tree, then, as the story progresses, place the other figures in a circular pattern as shown. As each character plays its part in the story's climax, remove it from the board. Finally, lift the tree just a bit and slide the babies out.

Baby Bird

Mother Bird

Mouse

Cat

Snake

Axe

Carpenter

Join Here

Elephant—Part One

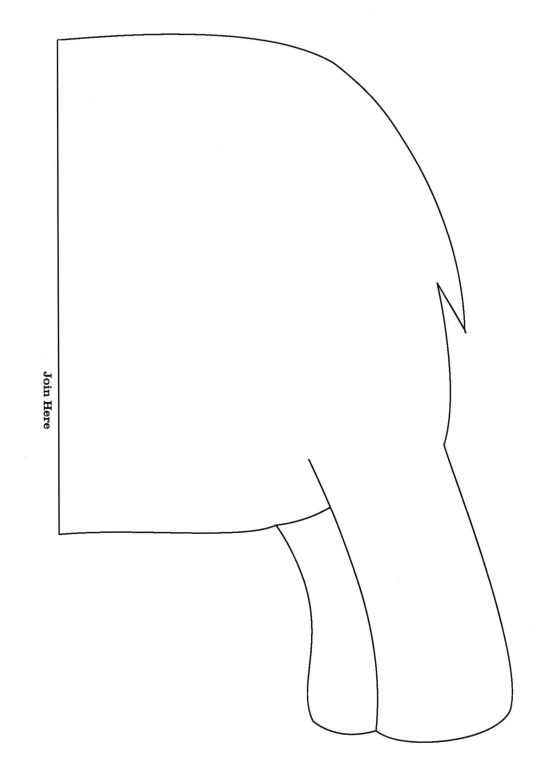

Join Here

Elephant—Part Two

THE BIRD AND HER BABIES
A Play for Readers' Theater

Nine characters and one narrator:

Mother Bird	Snake	Cat
Baby Birds (3)	Elephant	
Carpenter	Mouse	

NARRATOR: A bird once built a nest in a hollow tree and laid her eggs inside. When the baby birds hatched, they were hungry, and the mother bird worked from morning till night to feed them.

ALL BABY BIRDS: Cheep! Cheep! Cheep!

BABY BIRD 1: I'm hungry!

BABY BIRD 2: I'm hungry, too!

BABY BIRD 3: Feed me!

ALL BABY BIRDS: Cheep! Cheep! Cheep!

NARRATOR: The babies grew very fat. When it was time for them to leave the nest and learn to fly, they were too big to get out of the hole in the tree.

BABY BIRDS: (Sadly) Cheep, cheep, cheep.

MOTHER BIRD: Don't worry, my baby birds, I'll get you out. (To the carpenter) Carpenter, please cut this tree and make the hole bigger so that my babies can get out and learn to fly.

CARPENTER: No, why should I?

NARRATOR: Then the bird went to a see the snake.

MOTHER BIRD: Please bite the carpenter so that he will cut this tree and make the hole bigger. My babies can't get out and learn to fly.

SNAKE: No, why should I?

NARRATOR: Then the bird went to see the elephant.

MOTHER BIRD: Please step on the snake, so that she will bite the carpenter, so that he will cut this tree, so that my babies can get out and learn to fly.

ELEPHANT: No, why should I?

NARRATOR: Then the bird went to see the mouse.

MOTHER BIRD: Please tickle the inside of the elephant's trunk, so that he will step on the snake, so that she will bite the carpenter, so that he will cut this tree, so that my babies can get out and learn to fly.

MOUSE: No, why should I?

NARRATOR: Then the mother bird went to see the cat.

MOTHER BIRD: Please chase the mouse, so that she will tickle the elephant, so that he will step on the snake, so that she will bite the carpenter, so that he will cut this tree, so that my babies can get out and learn to fly.

CAT: Why shouldn't I? Chasing mice is what I do best! I will be happy to help you.

NARRATOR: Then the cat began to chase the mouse.

MOUSE: Stop! Stop!

NARRATOR: The mouse began to climb inside the elephant's trunk.

MOUSE: Tickle, tickle, tickle.

ELEPHANT: Hee! Hee! Hee! Stop! Stop!

NARRATOR: The elephant began to step on the snake.

SNAKE: Don't do it!

NARRATOR: The snake began to bite the carpenter.

CARPENTER: No! I'll cut the tree right now.

NARRATOR: And the carpenter cut the tree.

BABY BIRDS: Hooray! We're free!

MOTHER BIRD: Now fly off and find your own food, my dear little babies.

THE WOLF, THE GOAT, AND THE CABBAGES
An African Dilemma Tale

 task which seems at first impossible may be possible after all, if a person thinks about it in the right way. "The Wolf, the Goat, and the Cabbages" is a classic teaching tale that holds an important lesson: Sometimes when advancing toward a goal, it is necessary to do something that seems like a retreat. The tale has been told in many parts of Africa, especially the Swahili-speaking regions.

Once upon a time, a man traveled from his home to the city, taking a goat, a wolf, and a basket of cabbages with him to trade at the market. On his way, he came to a wide river. Now, there was a boat tied up on his side of the river, but it was a very small boat, only big enough to carry the man and one of the things he had with him. He would have to leave two things on the riverbank as he rowed the other across.

This presented a problem for the man. If he were to leave the goat with the cabbages, the goat would eat them. And if he were to leave the wolf with the goat, the wolf would eat it. Tell me, how did he get all three things across the river?

There are two possible solutions. When there is a choice of actions given for a particular number, follow either the (a)s or (b)s all the way through.

1.   The man took the goat across to the far side of the river, leaving the wolf with the cabbages on the near side.
2.   He left the goat on the far side of the river and rowed back.
3.   a.   He took the wolf across to the far side of the river and left them there.
     b.   He took the cabbages across to the far side of the river and left it there.
4.   He took the goat back to the near side of the river and left it there.
5.   a.   He took the cabbages across to the far side of the river.
     b.   He took the wolf across to the far side of the river.
6.   He left the wolf and the cabbages on the far side of the river and rowed back across.
7.   Finally, he took the goat across. Now all three things were on the far side of the river.

NOTES FOR FELTBOARD STORYTELLING

Make figures of the man, the boat, the wolf, the goat, and the basket of cabbages. The figures of the man, the goat, and the wolf should be two-sided. Make a river and the riverbanks from felt or foam and attach these firmly to the feltboard.

Goat

Man

Cabbages

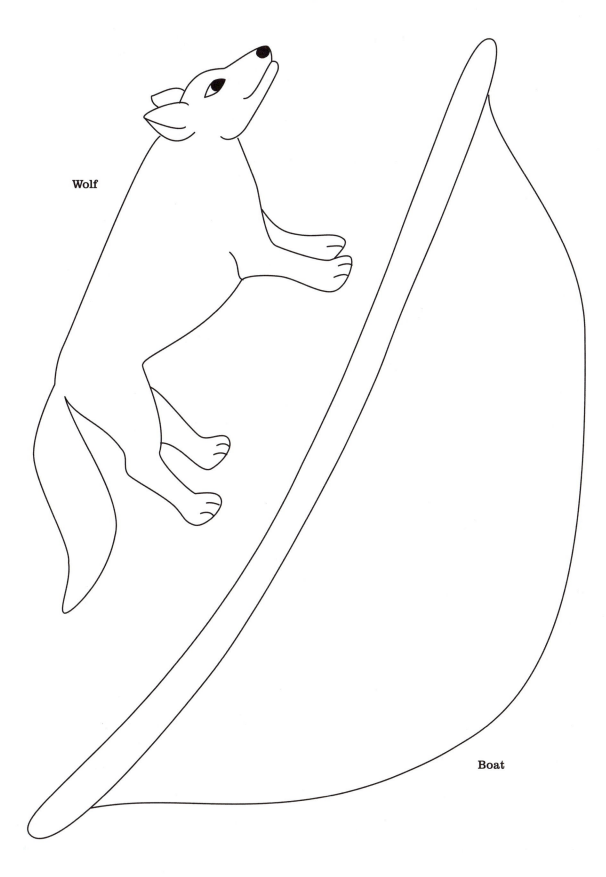

Wolf

Boat

THE WOLF, THE GOAT, AND THE CABBAGES
A Play for Readers' Theater

Six characters and one narrator

Man	**Goat**
Wolf	**Cabbages (3)**

NARRATOR: There was once a man who was traveling to market, and with him he had a wolf.

WOLF: Grrrr!

NARRATOR: And a goat.

GOAT: Beh-eh-eh-eh!

NARRATOR: And a basket, in which he carried several fat cabbages.

CABBAGE 1: Bounce.

CABBAGE 2: Bounce.

CABBAGE 3: Bounce.

NARRATOR: Soon they all came to a wide river.

MAN: How will I ever get across?

WOLF: There's a boat, silly.

MAN: But it's so small. We will make the boat sink.

GOAT: I think two of us could make it.

MAN: Good. I'll take the cabbages across first so that you won't eat them.

WOLF: What a good idea!

GOAT: Wait! If you leave me here with the wolf, he'll eat me.

MAN: I didn't think of that. I'll take you across, goat, and leave the wolf here with the cabbages.

WOLF: I wouldn't think of eating a cabbage.

CABBAGE 1, 2, AND 3: I wouldn't eat a wolf, either.

NARRATOR: So the man rowed the goat across the river, then he rowed back alone.

MAN: Which one of you shall I take now?

WOLF: Oh, take me, please. The cabbages will be an easy load to take last.

NARRATOR: Secretly, the wolf hoped the man would leave him with the goat. The man rowed the wolf across the river.

MAN: Now, just one more trip to get the cabbages.

WOLF: Yes, that's right. Go get the cabbages.

GOAT: No! Don't leave me here with the wolf. He will eat me. Take me back with you.

MAN: If I take you back, I'll never get everything across the river.

GOAT: Yes, you will. Try it and see.

NARRATOR: So the man took the goat back to the first side of the river and left him there. Then he took the cabbages across and left them with the wolf.

WOLF: I'm almost hungry enough to eat a cabbage. But not quite.

NARRATOR: The man rowed back across the river and picked up the goat.

MAN: I had to make more trips than I thought I would, but I got everything across the river, safe and sound.

GOAT: Beh-eh-eh-eh!

WOLF: Grrrr!

CABBAGE 1, 2, AND 3: Yea!

EAT, COAT, EAT!
A Turkish Folktale

In Turkey, many funny tales are told of Nasruddin Hodja. Although the Hodja often acts like a fool, he is really teaching people lessons about human nature. In the Turkish city of Eskishehr, where some say the Hodja was born, there is an annual Nasruddin festival. Everyone dresses up and acts out Hodja stories.

Once the Hodja was invited to a banquet at the home of a rich man. The rich man sent a messenger to see the Hodja. "Please come this afternoon," said the messenger. Now, the Hodja loved nothing better than a good dinner and a good audience for his stories and jokes. "This rich man must have heard about my fine wit and brilliant conversation," said the Hodja. So he set out for the banquet at once, without even bothering to wash up or change his clothes. He was wearing his everyday coat, which was really more patches than coat. Its only button hung by a single thread. His shirt showed through at both elbows. The coat was disreputable. When the Hodja arrived at the house where the banquet was being held, a servant stopped him at the gate.

"Where do you think you are going?" the servant asked him.

"Why, to the banquet, of course," answered the Hodja.

But the servant thought that the Hodja looked like a beggar. He refused to let him enter the banquet hall and sent him away with just a crust of stale bread.

"I believe I understand," remarked the Hodja, and he returned to his house and began looking through his clothes. "Ah! Here is my fine wool jacket with the silver and gold trim. I believe this will open the doors of the banquet hall."

The Hodja hurried back to the rich man's house, and the same servant met him at the gate. "Welcome, welcome," said the servant. "Come in. Let me seat you at the head table next to the master of the house."

The host greeted the Hodja warmly. "I have heard much about you, Nasruddin Hodja," he said. "The soup has just been served. Eat, my honored guest."

The Hodja took a bowl of soup. He opened the sleeve of his coat and poured the soup into it. "Eat, coat, eat!" the Hodja said.

"What is he doing?" the host asked the other guests.

They assured him that the Hodja often did strange things like this.

The Hodja took a cup of wine and poured it into his other sleeve, saying, "Drink, coat, drink!"

At last the host was overcome by curiosity. "Nasruddin Hodja, may I ask what you are doing?"

"It seems," said the Hodja, "that my *coat* was invited to this banquet, not I. Therefore, I am feeding my coat."

NOTES FOR FELTBOARD STORYTELLING

Make figures of the Hodja, the messenger, the servant, the rich man, and the guest. Props include the Hodja's good jacket, a banquet table, a bowl, and a goblet. As a feltboard story, "Eat, Coat, Eat!" has two scenes. When the story begins, place the Hodja and the messenger on the feltboard. Then remove them and place the banquet scenery—table, food, and guests—near the top of the board. These will remain in place for the rest of the story. The Hodja encounters the servant at the lower part of the board. The Hodja changes his coat "offstage"; you simply remove him from the board then return him a moment later wearing his good jacket. Pick up the bowl and goblet with the very tips of your fingers, holding each near one of the Hodja's sleeves as he says, "Eat, coat, eat," and "Drink, coat, drink!"

Hodja

Coat

Messenger

Servant

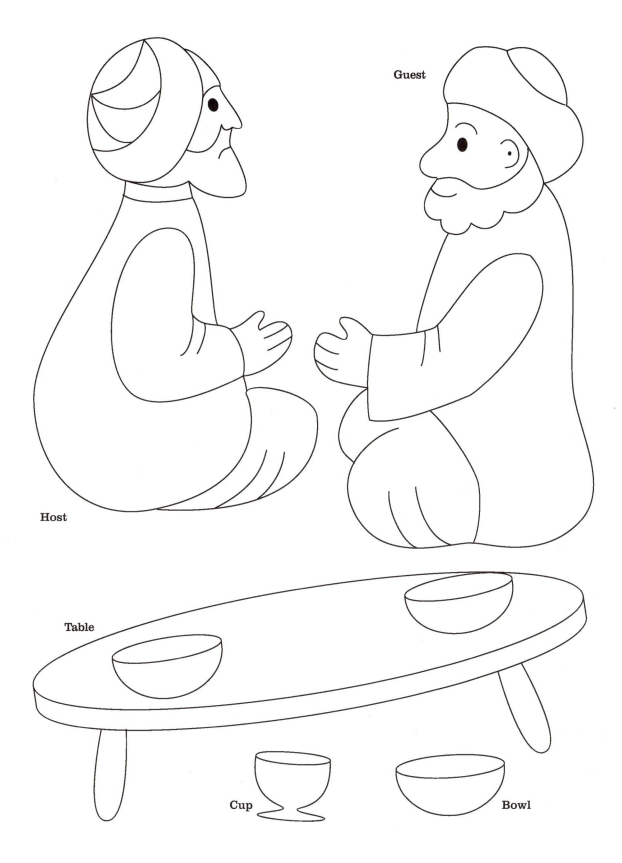

Guest

Host

Table

Cup

Bowl

EAT, COAT, EAT!
A Play for Readers' Theater

Five characters and one narrator

Hodja	**Host**
Messenger	**Guest**
Servant	

MESSENGER: Excuse me. Are you Nasruddin Hodja?

HODJA: I am.

MESSENGER: You are invited to a banquet this afternoon at the great house on the hilltop.

HODJA: The owner of that house is a rich man. No doubt he has heard of my great wit and brilliant conversation. I shall leave at once for the banquet.

NARRATOR: The Hodja left without even bothering to wash up or change his clothes. He was wearing his everyday coat, which was really more patches than coat. Its only button hung by a single thread. His shirt showed through at both elbows. He looked disreputable. When he arrived at the house where the banquet was being held, a servant stopped him at the gate.

SERVANT: Where do you think you are going?

HODJA: I have been invited to this banquet.

SERVANT: I don't think so. You look like a beggar. Here, take this bread and go away.

HODJA: But . . . I . . . was . . .

SERVANT: Goodbye.

HODJA: . . . invited!

NARRATOR: The servant closed the gate. The Hodja returned to his house.

HODJA: Ah! Here is my wool jacket with the silver and gold trim.

NARRATOR: He hurried back to the banquet. The same servant met him at the gate.

SERVANT: Welcome, welcome. Come in. Let me seat you at the head table next to the master of the house.

HOST: Greetings! I have heard much about you, Nasruddin Hodja. The soup has just been served. Eat, my honored guest.

HODJA: Thank you, thank you.

NARRATOR: The Hodja took a bowl of soup. He opened the sleeve of his coat, and poured the soup into it.

HODJA: Eat, coat, eat!

HOST: What is he doing?

GUEST: I have heard that the Hodja often does strange things like this.

NARRATOR: The Hodja took a cup of wine and poured it into his other sleeve.

HODJA: Drink, coat, drink!

HOST: Nasruddin Hodja, may I ask what you are doing?

HODJA: You did not invite me to the banquet. You invited my coat. And so, I am feeding my coat.

THE LITTLE ANT
A Spanish Folktale

The tale of the beautiful little ant, cockroach, or butterfly, who finds a coin, makes herself beautiful, and wins a husband, is widely known in Spain, France, and Italy, as well as in the Spanish-speaking areas of the Americas.

Once upon a time, there was a little ant, a pretty ant, an ant who found a silver coin on the ground.

"Oh! What shall I buy with this coin?" she mused. "Shall I buy a loaf of bread? No, I would eat it, and soon it would be gone. A sweet cake? No, I would eat it, too, and soon it would be gone."

The little ant sat and thought and thought and thought. At last she had an idea. She would go to town and buy herself a silk dress, a lace shawl, and pretty leather boots. When she had done that, she put on her new clothes and sat in front of her house.

A rooster walked up to her door. "Oh, little ant," said the rooster, "how pretty you are! Will you marry me?"

"Perhaps I will marry you," said the little ant. "Tell me how you will sing to me after we are married."

"I will sing to you like this," the rooster told her. "Coquerico! Coquerico!"

"No, no, no!" cried the little ant. "That is much too loud and frightening. I cannot marry you."

The rooster walked away sadly, his tail feathers drooping.

Next, a duck came waddling cheerfully to her door.

"Oh, little ant," quacked the duck, "how lovely you are. Will you marry me?"

"Perhaps I will marry you," said the little ant. "Tell me how you will sing to me after we are married."

"I will sing to you like this," the duck said. "Cuá, cuá, cuá!"

"No, no, no!" cried the little ant. "That is much too sad and dreary. I cannot marry you."

The duck waddled away sadly, wiping his tears with his wingtips.

Next, a cricket, hopped to the little ant's door.

"Oh, little ant," chirped the cricket, "how charming you are. Will you marry me?"

"Perhaps I will marry you," said the little ant. "But first, tell me how you will sing to me after we are married."

"I will sing to you like this," said the cricket. "Pío, pío, pío!"

"No, no, no!" cried the little ant. "That is much too boring. I cannot marry you."

The cricket hopped away, sobbing sadly.

Then, along came a mouse, scurrying along the road, wearing his finest coat, his whiskers neatly combed.

"Oh, little ant," he sang, "how elegant you are. Will you marry me?"

"Perhaps I will marry you," said the little ant. "But first, tell me how you will sing to me after we are married."

"Like this," said the mouse. "Cuii, cuii, cuii!"

"Oh, I like your song," said the little ant. "Yes, I will marry you."

So the ant and the mouse were married. Everyone came and danced at their wedding, and they all sang together:

Cuii, cuii, cuii!

Pío, pío, pío!

Cuá, cuá, cuá!

Coquerico! Coquerico!

NOTES FOR FELTBOARD STORYTELLING

Make figures of the rooster, the duck, the cricket, the mouse, the two different figures of the little ant, and a little round coin. The story works well without scenery, especially if the figures are large in relation to the feltboard. If you wish, make a house for the little ant with a balcony where she can sit as she questions her suitors.

Rooster

Cricket

Duck

Little Ant (fancy)

Little Ant (plain)

81

Mouse

THE LITTLE ANT
A Play for Readers' Theater

Five characters and one narrator

Little ant   **Duck**   **Mouse**

Rooster   **Cricket**

NARRATOR: Once upon a time, there was a little ant, a pretty ant, an ant who found a silver coin on the ground.

LITTLE ANT: Oh! What shall I buy with this coin? Shall I buy a loaf of bread? No. I would eat it, and soon it would be gone. A sweet cake? No, I would eat it, and soon it would be gone.

NARRATOR: The little ant sat and thought and thought and thought. At last, she had an idea.

LITTLE ANT: I will go to town and buy myself a silk dress, a lace shawl, and pretty leather boots.

NARRATOR: And she did. Then she put on her new clothes and sat in front of her house. Soon, along came a rooster.

ROOSTER: Oh, little ant, how pretty you are! Will you marry me?

LITTLE ANT: Perhaps I will marry you. Tell me how you will sing to me after we are married.

ROOSTER: Coquerico! Coquerico!

LITTLE ANT: No, no, no! That is much too loud and frightening. I cannot marry you.

NARRATOR: The rooster walked away sadly, his tail feathers drooping.

ROOSTER: Boo hoo! Boo hoo!

NARRATOR: Next, along came a duck.

DUCK: Oh, little ant, how lovely you are. Will you marry me?

LITTLE ANT: Perhaps I will marry you. Tell me how you will sing to me after we are married.

DUCK: Cuá, cuá, cuá!

83

LITTLE ANT: No, no, no! That is much too sad and dreary. I cannot marry you.

NARRATOR: The duck waddled away, wiping his tears.

DUCK: Boo hoo! Boo hoo!

NARRATOR: Next, along came a cricket.

CRICKET: Oh, little ant, how charming you are. Will you marry me?

LITTLE ANT: Perhaps I will marry you. Tell me how you will sing to me after we are married.

CRICKET: Pío, pío, pío!

LITTLE ANT: No, no, no! That is much too boring. I cannot marry you.

NARRATOR: The cricket hopped away, weeping and sobbing.

DUCK: Boo hoo! Boo hoo!

NARRATOR: Next, along came a mouse.

MOUSE: Oh, little ant, how elegant you are. Will you marry me?

LITTLE ANT: Perhaps I will marry you. Tell me how you will sing to me after we are married.

MOUSE: Cuii, cuii, cuii!

LITTLE ANT: Oh, I like your song. Yes, I will marry you.

NARRATOR: So the ant and the mouse were married. Everyone came and danced at their wedding, and they all sang together.

MOUSE: Cuii, cuii, cuii!

CRICKET: Pío, pío, pío!

DUCK: Cuá, cuá, cuá!

ROOSTER: Coquerico! Coquerico!

10

MUNACHAR AND MANACHAR
An Irish Folktale

No one really knows what a Munachar or a Manachar is—they seem to be small, argumentative beings, a bit like leprechauns. Chain tales like this one exist in the folklore of many countries. Two examples are "The Bird and Her Babies" from India and the Cuban folktale, "The Two Monkeys," both in this book. A chain tale features a character who needs to get something done and who asks a series of people, animals, and even objects to help, setting up a humorous chain reaction.

There once lived a Munachar and a Manachar, a long time ago, and it is a long time since it was, and if they were alive now, they would not be alive then. One day, they went out together to pick raspberries. Munachar picked the raspberries, and Manachar ate the raspberries. So Munachar decided he must get a rod, and bind it across Manachar's mouth so that Manachar couldn't eat anything at all.

Munachar found a rod.

"What news today?" asked the rod.

85

Munachar answered,

It's my own news I'm seeking.

Going looking for a rod,

A rod to stop Manachar from eating my raspberries, every one.

"You will not get me," said the rod, "until you get an axe to cut me."

Munachar came to an axe.

"What news today?" asked the axe.

Munachar answered,

It's my own news I'm seeking.

Going looking for an axe,

An axe to cut a rod,

A rod to stop Manachar from eating my raspberries, every one.

"You will not get me," said the axe, "until you get a stone to sharpen me."

Munachar came to a stone.

"What news today?" said the stone.

Munachar answered,

It's my own news I'm seeking.

Going looking for a stone,

A stone to sharpen an axe,

An axe to cut a rod,

A rod to stop Manachar from eating my raspberries, every one.

"You will not get me," said the stone, "until you get water to wet me."

Munachar came to some water.

"What news today?" said the water.

Munachar answered,

It's my own news I'm seeking.

Going looking for some water,

Water to wet a stone,

A stone to sharpen an axe,

An axe to cut a rod,

A rod to stop Manachar from eating my raspberries, every one.

"You'll not get me," said the water, "until you get a deer to swim in me."

Munachar came to a deer.

"What news today?" said the deer.

Munachar answered,

It's my own news I'm seeking.

Going looking for a deer,

A deer to swim in the water,

Water to wet a stone,

A stone to sharpen an axe,

An axe to cut a rod,
A rod to stop Manachar from eating my raspberries, every one.

"You'll not get me," said the deer, "until you get a hound to chase me."
Munachar came to a hound.
"What news today?" said the hound.
Munachar answered,

It's my own news I'm seeking.
Going looking for a hound,
A hound to chase a deer,
A deer to swim in some water,
Water to wet a stone,
A stone to sharpen an axe,
An axe to cut a rod,
A rod to stop Manachar from eating my raspberries, every one.

"You'll not get me," said the hound, "until you get a bit of butter to put in my claw."
Munachar came to some butter.
"What news today?" said the butter.
Munachar answered,

It's my own news I'm seeking.
Going looking for some butter,
Butter to go in the claw of a hound,
A hound to chase a deer,
A deer to swim in the water,
Water to wet a stone,
A stone to sharpen an axe,
An axe to cut a rod,
A rod to stop Manachar from eating my raspberries, every one.

"You'll not get me," said the butter, "until you get a cat to lick me."
Munachar came to a cat.
"What news today?" said the cat.
Munachar answered,

It's my own news I'm seeking.
Going looking for a cat,
A cat to lick some butter,
Butter to go in the claw of a hound,
A hound to chase a deer,
A deer to swim in the water,
Water to wet a stone,
A stone to sharpen an axe,

An axe to cut a rod,
A rod to stop Manachar from eating my raspberries, every one.

"I'd certainly like a lick of butter," replied the cat.

Munachar took the cat to the butter, and the cat licked the butter, and the butter went into the claw of the hound, and the hound chased the deer, and the deer swam in the water, and the water wet the stone, and the stone sharpened the axe, and the axe cut the rod, and Munachar took the rod to Manachar. He wanted to put the rod across Manachar's mouth, but when he found Manachar, Manachar had eaten so many raspberries that he had BURST!

NOTES FOR FELTBOARD STORYTELLING

Make figures of Munachar, thin Manachar, fat Manachar, the raspberry bushes, the rod, the axe, the stone, the water, the deer, the hound, the butter, and the cat.

Begin telling the tale by placing Munachar, thin Manachar, and the raspberry bushes at the top center of the feltboard (if you write their names on their hats, you won't confuse Munachar and Manachar during storytelling). Remove thin Manachar from the feltboard at the point when Munachar goes off to find a rod. Add the feltboard figures as they are mentioned in the tale, and remove each as it plays its part in the final chain reaction. For example:

. . . and the cat licked the butter (remove cat), and the butter went into the claw of the hound (remove butter), and so on.

Munachar needs an axe to cut the rod because it is too long. When he finally cuts it, pick it up and fold it in half to show that it is now smaller. Hold it in one hand until the story is finished. After Munachar gets the rod, place the fat Manachar on the board, removing him when he BURSTS.

Fat Manachar

Hound

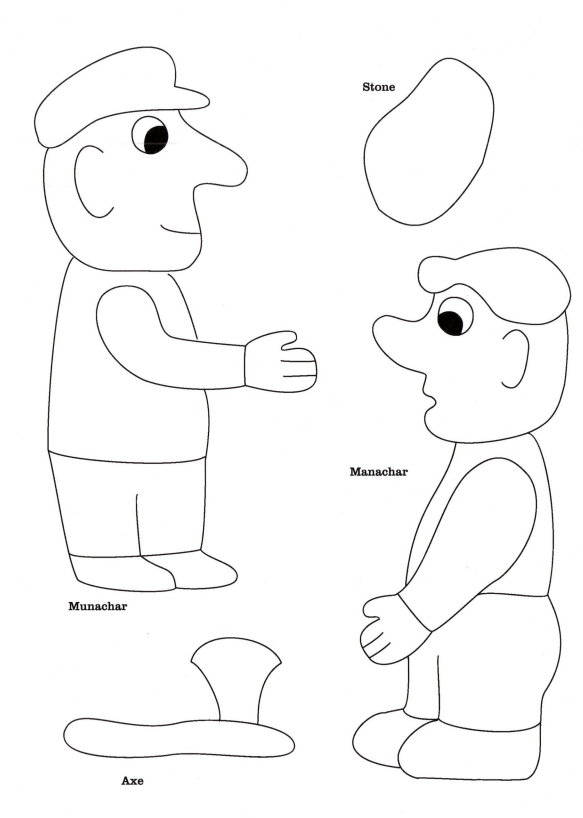

Stone

Manachar

Munachar

Axe

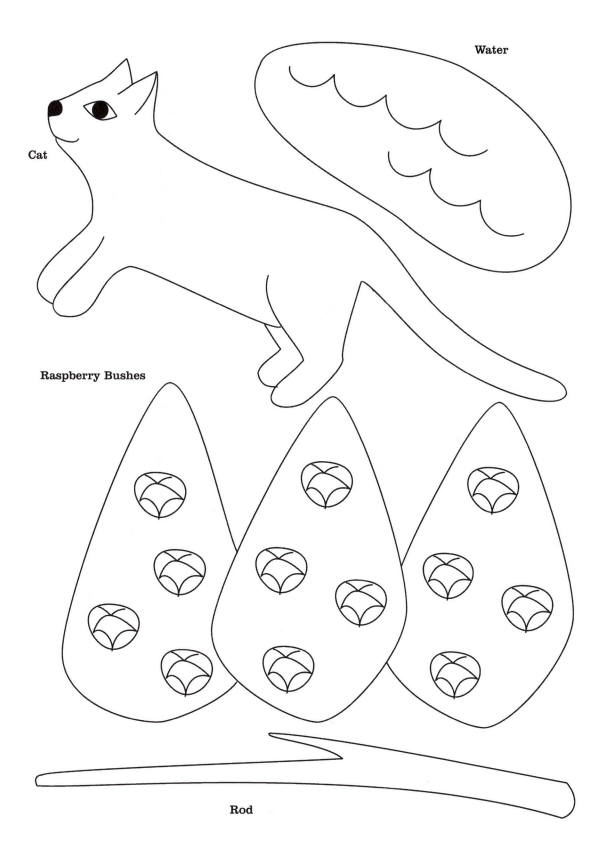

Water

Cat

Raspberry Bushes

Rod

Butter Churn

Deer

MUNACHAR AND MANACHAR
A Play for Readers' Theater

Ten characters and a narrator

Munachar	**Stone**	**Butter**
Manachar	**Water**	**Cat**
Rod	**Deer**	
Axe	**Hound**	

NARRATOR: There once lived a Munachar and a Manachar, a long time ago, and it is a long time since it was, and if they were alive now, they would not be alive then. One day, they went out together to pick raspberries. Munachar picked the raspberries, and Manachar ate the raspberries.

MUNACHAR: Stop eating my raspberries.

MANACHAR: Mphghbh.

MUNACHAR: I am going to get a rod and bind it across your mouth so that you can't eat MY raspberries. Ah, here's a nice rod.

ROD: What news today, Munachar?

MUNACHAR: It's my own news I'm seeking.
　　　　Going looking for a rod,
　　　　A rod to stop Manachar from eating my
　　　　　raspberries, every one.

ROD: You will not get me until you get an axe to cut me.

MUNACHAR: Here's a nice axe.

AXE: What news today, Munachar?

MUNACHAR: It's my own news I'm seeking.
　　　　Going looking for an axe,
　　　　An axe to cut a rod,
　　　　A rod to stop Manachar from eating my
　　　　　raspberries, every one.

AXE: You will not get me until you get a stone to sharpen me.

MUNACHAR: Here's a nice stone.

STONE: What news today, Munachar?

MUNACHAR: It's my own news I'm seeking.
Going looking for a stone,
A stone to sharpen an axe,
An axe to cut a rod,
A rod to stop Manachar from eating my
raspberries, every one.

STONE: You will not get me until you get water to wet me.

MUNACHAR: Here's some nice water.

WATER: What news today, Munachar?

MUNACHAR: It's my own news I'm seeking.
Going looking for some water,
Water to wet a stone,
A stone to sharpen an axe,
An axe to cut a rod,
A rod to stop Manachar from eating my
raspberries, every one.

WATER: You'll not get me until you get a deer to swim in me.

MUNACHAR: Here's a nice deer.

DEER: What news today, Munachar?

MUNACHAR: It's my own news I'm seeking.
Going looking for a deer,
A deer to swim in some water,
Water to wet a stone,
A stone to sharpen an axe,
An axe to cut a rod,
A rod to stop Manachar from eating my
raspberries, every one.

DEER: You'll not get me until you get a hound to chase me.

MUNACHAR: Here's a nice hound.

HOUND: What news today, Munachar?

MUNACHAR: It's my own news I'm seeking.
Going looking for a hound,
A hound to chase a deer,
A deer to swim in some water,
Water to wet a stone,
A stone to sharpen an axe,
An axe to cut a rod,
A rod to stop Manachar from eating my
　raspberries, every one.

HOUND: You'll not get me until you get a bit of butter to put in my claw.

MUNACHAR: Here's a nice bit of butter.

BUTTER: What news today, Munachar?

MUNACHAR: It's my own news I'm seeking.
Going looking for a bit of butter,
Butter to put in the claw of a hound,
A hound to chase a deer,
A deer to swim in the water,
Water to wet a stone,
A stone to sharpen an axe,
An axe to cut a rod,
A rod to stop Manachar from eating my
　raspberries, every one.

BUTTER: You'll not get me until you get a cat to lick me.

MUNACHAR: Here's a nice cat.

CAT: What news today, Munachar?

MUNACHAR: It's my own news I'm seeking.
Going looking for a cat,
A cat to lick some butter,
Butter to go in the claw of a hound,
A hound to chase a deer,
A deer to swim in some water,
Water to wet a stone,
A stone to sharpen an axe,
An axe to cut a rod,
A rod to stop Manachar from eating my
　raspberries, every one.

CAT: I'd like a lick of butter.

NARRATOR: Munachar led the cat to the butter,

And the cat licked the butter,

And the butter went into the claw of the hound,

And the hound chased the deer,

And the deer swam in the water,

And the water wet the stone,

And the stone sharpened the axe,

And the axe cut the rod.

Munachar took the rod and ran to the place where he had left Manachar. But when he found Manachar, Manachar had eaten so many raspberries that he had . . .

MANACHAR: mmm . . . *mmm* . . . MMM . . .

EVERYONE: BURST!

11

THE WEE BANNOCK
A Scottish Folktale

A bannock is a loaf of bread baked on an iron griddle over an open fire. This tale is the Scottish cousin of the American "Gingerbread Man" and the English "Johnny Cake." The wee bannock meets the same fate as these and other naughty cookies found in world folklore.

A woman was baking a bannock, and there was an old man who wanted it, so he said, "Your bannock is burning. Come away and I'll turn it."

And the woman said, "No, I'll turn it."

"No, I'll turn it," says he.

"I'll just turn myself," said the bannock. It turned over and then turned around and whirled out the door. The man and the woman ran after it. One flung a pot at it and the other flung a pan, but on and on and on it ran.

Soon, the bannock came to a dog. "Welcome, welcome, wee bannockie," said the dog. "Where have you come from?"

"I outran

    a wee wee woman and a wee wee man,

A wee wee pot and a wee wee pan,
And I'll outrun you, too, if I can."

And the dog ran and ran, but she couldn't catch the wee bannock. The bannock came to a pig. "Welcome, welcome, wee bannockie," said she. "Where have you come from?"

"I outran

a wee wee woman and a wee wee man,
A wee wee pot and a wee wee pan,
And a dog,
And I'll outrun you, too, if I can."

And the pig ran and ran, but she couldn't catch the wee bannock. The bannock came to a sheep. "Welcome, welcome, wee bannockie," said he. "Where have you come from?"

"I outran

a wee wee woman and a wee wee man,
A wee wee pot and a wee wee pan,
And a dog,
And a pig,
And I'll outrun you, too, if I can."

And the sheep ran and ran, but he couldn't catch the wee bannock. The bannock came to a stream, and there sat a sly old fox. "Welcome, welcome, wee bannockie," said the fox. "Where have you come from?"

"I outran

a wee wee woman and a wee wee man,
A wee wee pot and a wee wee pan,
And a dog,
And a pig,
And a sheep,
And I'll outrun you, too, if I can."

The fox licked his lips. "Why don't you hop onto my back," he said, "and I'll give you a ride across the stream."

"No, I'll keep on running," said the bannock.

"No, no," said the fox. "Just get on my back, and I'll carry you across the stream."

So the bannock got on his back. and as the fox began to swim the stream, he turned his head around and took a wee bite out of the bannock.

"Oh, you're nippin' us, you're nippin' us!" cried the bannock.

"No, I'm just scratching my back," the fox replied, and he took another bite.

"Oh, you're nippin' us, you're nippin' us!" cried the bannock again.

The fox took another bite, and another, the crumbs falling into the stream. And that was the end of the wee bannock.

NOTES FOR FELTBOARD STORYTELLING

Make figures of the wee bannock, the woman, the man, the fireplace, the dog, the pig, the sheep, and the fox. Cut a piece of blue felt or foam to represent the stream. There are no figures for the pot and pan—they are described but not shown. To show the chase, simply have the chaser(s) and the wee bannock on the feltboard, and remove the chaser(s) when the bannock outruns them. The fox can appear to nibble at the bannock if you make him (the fox) two-sided and fold his head backwards as he nips at it.

Man

Woman

Pig

Wee Bannock

Dog

Sheep

Fox

Fireplace

THE WEE BANNOCK
A Play for Readers' Theater

Seven characters and two narrators

Woman	**Dog**	**Fox**
Man	**Pig**	
Wee Bannock	**Sheep**	

NARRATOR 1: A woman was baking a bannock.

NARRATOR 2: And there was an old man who wanted to eat it.

MAN: Your bannock is burning! Your bannock is burning! Let me turn it over.

WOMAN: No, I'll turn it.

MAN: No, I'll turn it.

WOMAN: No, I'll turn it.

MAN: No, I'll turn it.

WEE BANNOCK: Hee, hee. Don't fight over me! I'll just turn myself.

NARRATOR 1: The bannock turned over and then turned around and whirled out the door. The man and the woman ran after it. One flung a pot at it, and the other flung a pan.

NARRATOR 2: But on and on and on it ran until it came to a dog.

DOG: Welcome, welcome, wee bannockie. Where have you come from?

WEE BANNOCK: I outran a wee wee woman and a wee wee man,
A wee wee pot and a wee wee pan,
And I'll outrun you, too, if I can.

NARRATOR 1: And the dog ran and ran, but she couldn't catch the wee bannock.

NARRATOR 2: Then the wee bannock came to a pig.

PIG: Welcome, welcome, wee bannockie. Where have you come from?

WEE BANNOCK: I outran a wee wee woman and a wee wee man,
A wee wee pot and a wee wee pan,
And a dog,
And I'll outrun you, too, if I can.

NARRATOR 1: And the pig ran and ran, but she couldn't catch the wee bannock.

NARRATOR 2: The bannock came to a hungry sheep.

SHEEP: Welcome, welcome, wee bannockie. Where have you come from?

WEE BANNOCK: I outran a wee wee woman and a wee wee man,
A wee wee pot and a wee wee pan,
And a dog,
And a pig,
And I'll outrun you, too, if I can.

NARRATOR 1: The sheep ran and ran, but he couldn't catch the wee bannock.

NARRATOR 2: Next the bannock came to a stream, and there sat a sly old fox.

FOX: Welcome, welcome, wee bannockie. Where have you come from?

WEE BANNOCK: I outran a wee wee woman and a wee wee man,
A wee wee pot and a wee wee pan,
And a dog,
And a pig,
And a sheep,
And I'll outrun you, too, if I can.

FOX: Why don't you hop onto my back, and I'll give you a ride across the stream.

WEE BANNOCK: No, I'll keep on running, thank you.

FOX: No, no, just get on my back, and I'll carry you across the stream.

NARRATOR 1: So the bannock got on his back, and the fox began to swim across the stream.

NARRATOR 2: The fox turned its head around and took a wee bite out of the bannock.

FOX: (Smacking his lips) Mmmmmm.

WEE BANNOCK: Oh, you're nippin' us, you're nippin' us!

FOX: No, I'm just scratching my back.

NARRATOR 1: And he took another bite.

Fox: (Smacking his lips) Mmmmm.

Wee Bannock: Oh, you're nippin' us, you're nippin' us again!

Narrator 1: The fox took another bite, and another, and the crumbs fell into the stream.

Narrator 2: And that was the end of the wee bannock.

12

THE TRICKS OF A FOX
A Folktale of the Koryak People of Siberia

Folktales of an animal who cannot swim, crossing water by persuading water creatures to form a bridge, are common throughout Asia. In Indonesia, for example, the trickster is Kanchil, the mouse deer, and the dupes are crocodiles. In Japanese tales, it is a hare who tricks either crocodiles or sharks. In this tale, a fox tricks all the creatures in the sea by pretending to be a powerful shaman.

One morning, the fox's children were hungry, so their father went out to find something for them to eat. Looking up, he saw an eagle sitting on her treetop nest. The fox imagined that eagle eggs might make a tasty breakfast, so he made up a plan to trick the eagle into throwing down her eggs to him.

The fox found some long sticks and put some in each ear. He looked like he had horns. "I look like a powerful animal now," he bragged. He shook his head back and forth as he called to the eagle, "Hey! Throw me an egg, or I'll knock down your tree."

Now, the eagle knew right away that it was the fox, but she pretended to be afraid. "What terrible creature are you?" she asked.

"I am the Great Eagle Eater!" cried the fox.

"Oh, I'm so scared!" the eagle answered. "Stay right there, Great Eagle Eater, and I'll fly down with an egg for you."

The fox was quite pleased with himself until he felt sharp talons grip his back. The eagle grabbed him and carried him far out to sea. She dropped him onto a tiny island and flew away with a screech of laughter.

"I should have known better than to try to trick an eagle," moaned the fox. "Now I have to figure out a way to get back home again." The fox began to walk back and forth and to sing a shaman's song.

> Are there more animals in the sea?
> Are there more animals on land?
> Are there more animals in the sea?
> Are there more animals on land?

Soon, all the creatures of the sea swam to that island.

"There are more animals in the sea, of course," said a walrus.

Why don't you count us?" said a shark.

"I can't see you. The fox complained, You are all hiding under the water."

Then even more sea creatures came to the surface, crying "Here we are! What do you think now?"

"There are truly very many of you," the fox told them. "But how can I count you?"

"I've heard you're very smart," said a whale. "You will think of a way."

"You must all get in one long line," said the fox. Please line up from here to the mainland."

So the sea creatures formed a long line. There were whales and walruses, seals and sharks. The fox skipped quickly across their backs, counting one, two, three, four, five, six, seven . . . .

As he was just about to hop off the last animal in line, the fox snapped up a fat fish from the shallow water and took it home to feed his children. He never did tell the sea creatures how many of them he had counted.

NOTES FOR FELTBOARD STORYTELLING

The figures for telling this tale with the feltboard should be fairly small, since so many need to be "onstage" at the end of the story. Make figures of the fox, the cubs, the eagle, the whale, the walrus, the seal, the shark, the sticks the fox puts in his ears, and the fish he takes home to his cubs. Make as many more creatures as necessary in order to form a line across the feltboard—either from duplicates of the patterns or from your own research. Scenery includes the fox's den, the eagle's tree, the sea, and the island. Design these to fit your feltboard, using the figure below as a model.

Eagle

Fish

Fox Cubs

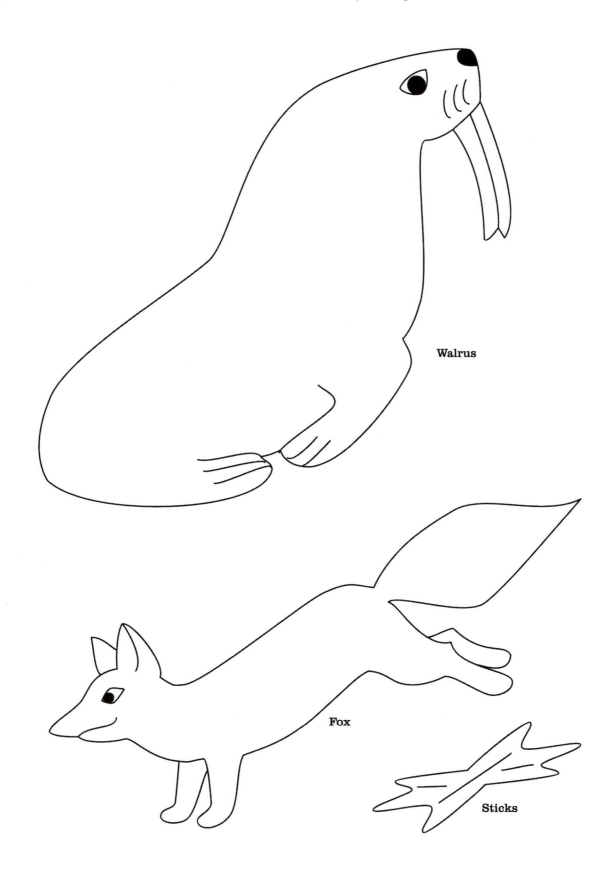

Walrus

Fox

Sticks

Whale

Shark

Seal

THE TRICKS OF A FOX
A Play for Readers' Theater

Eight to ten characters and two narrators

Fox	**Shark**	**Whale**
Fox cubs (2 to 4)	**Seal**	
Eagle	**Walrus**	

NARRATOR 1: The fox cubs were hungry.

FOX CUBS: Daddy! Daddy! Bring us something to eat. We're starving.

NARRATOR 2: So the fox set out to find food for them. Looking up, he saw an eagle in her nest.

FOX: Eagle eggs would make a good meal for my family. A fox can't climb a tree, but a fox knows how to use his brain. I think I can trick that eagle and make her throw down her eggs to me.

NARRATOR 1: The fox found some long sticks and put a few in each ear.

NARRATOR 2: He looked like he had horns.

FOX: (To himself) I look like a powerful animal now. (To the eagle) Hey, Eagle! Throw me an egg, or I'll knock down your tree.

EAGLE: (To herself) That silly fox. He think's I'm a fool. (To the fox) What terrible creature are you?

FOX: I am the Great Eagle Eater!

EAGLE: (Pretending to be frightened) Oh, I'm so scared! Stay right there, Great Eagle Eater, and I'll fly down with an egg for you.

NARRATOR 1: The fox was feeling quite pleased with himself until he felt sharp talons in his back.

NARRATOR 2: He was lifted up into the air. The eagle carried him far out to sea. She dropped him onto a tiny island.

FOX: Wait! Don't leave me here. There's no food here.

NARRATOR 2: The eagle flew off with a screech of laughter.

EAGLE: Screeeeeech! Screeeeeech!

114

Fox: Well, I guess I should have known better than to try to trick an eagle. Now I have to figure out a way to get home.

Narrator 1: The fox began to walk back and forth, singing a shaman's song.

Fox: Are there more animals in the sea?
Are there more animals on land?
Are there more animals in the sea?
Are there more animals on land?

Narrator 1: Soon all the creatures of the sea swam to that island. A whale called out—

Whale: There are more animals in the sea, of course.

Narrator 2: Then a shark shouted—

Shark: Why don't you count us?

Fox: I can't see you all. You are hiding under the water.

Narrator 1: Then every sea creature came to the surface.

Seal: Here we are!

Walrus: What do you think now?

Fox: Yes, there are a lot of you. But how can I count you?

Shark: I've heard you're very smart. Think of a way.

Fox: I know. You must all get into one long line. Please line up from here to the mainland.

Narrator 1: So the sea creatures formed a long line. There were whales and walruses, seals and sharks.

Narrator 2: The fox skipped quickly across their backs.

Fox: One, two, three, four, five, six, seven . . . da-ta-ta-ta da-ta-ta-ta . . . one-hundred thirty eight, one-hundred thirty nine . . .

Narrator 1: As he was just about to hop off the last sea animal, the fox snapped up a fat fish from the shallow water and took it home to feed his children.

Narrator 2: And he never did tell the sea creatures how many of them he had counted.

13

THROUGH THE NEEDLE'S EYE
An Inuit Folktale

This tale of a great swallower is similar to other stories in world folklore about people and animals who go about gulping everything in sight. Often, these characters have been spoiled and overfed at home and as a result can't control their appetites. Many meet sad ends, like this Inuit boy who bursts while trying to go through the eye of his grandmother's needle.

Once upon a time, there was a boy who lived with his grandmother in a little house near the sea. The boy was always hungry. At last, he had eaten every last bit of food in the house but was still hungry.

"Well," said his grandmother, "you'll just have to go out and hunt for something to eat."

So he went out, and he walked along the sea, and the first thing he found was a big fish. He picked it up and swallowed it whole. *Slurrrrp!*

Then he saw a seal, and he thought he'd just eat that, too. He swallowed it down, whiskers and all. *Slurrrrp!*

Then he saw a walrus, and he thought he'd just eat that, too. He swallowed it down, tusks and all. *Slurrrrp!*

Then he saw something really big. Something really, really big. It was a whale. *Slurrrrp!* Yes, he ate that, too. Blubber and all.

All that eating made him thirsty, so he looked around for something to drink. The ocean was too salty, he thought, so he walked to a lake. *Slurrrrp!* Yes, he drank the lake. Then he walked back to his grandmother's house, but he had eaten so much, he couldn't get through the door.

"Grandma," he said, "I can't get through the door."

"Why don't you come in through the window," she said.

He tried and tried, but he couldn't squeeze through the window.

"Grandma," he said, "I can't get through the window, either."

"Why don't you come in through the chimney," she said.

He tried and tried, but he couldn't get through the chimney.

"Grandma," he said, "I can't get in through the chimney, either."

"Then you'll just have to come in through the eye of my needle," she said, and she held her hand out the door. The boy squeezed himself through the eye of his grandmother's needle and—*kaboom!*—he exploded.

Where the house had been, there was now a lake, and in the lake there were a fish, a seal, a walrus, and a whale swimming around and around. But no one ever saw that boy or his grandmother again.

NOTES FOR FELTBOARD STORYTELLING

Make the figures of the fish, seal, walrus, and whale from patterns given with the previous tale, "The Tricks of a Fox." Make the grandmother and the two figures of the boy (thin and fat). Make the reverse side of the fat boy from light-blue felt: this figure doubles as the boy and the lake he drinks. Make the house from felt and cut the door along the side and top so that it can open. Then glue the house, except the door, to a piece of interfacing. Behind the door, on the interfacing, draw the grandmother's arm and hand holding the needle.

Begin telling the story with the house at the upper right of the feltboard, placing the boy and his grandmother in front of it. When the boy goes hunting, remove the grandmother. As the boy encounters each animal, position it on the feltboard next to him, taking it off as soon as he eats it. After he drinks the lake, turn the lake over and remove the first figure of the boy. When the grandmother tells the boy to go through the eye of her needle, open the door to the house so that the children can see her arm. When the boy explodes,

117

turn the two-sided figure over so that it once again becomes the lake. Quickly remove the house and place the sea creatures on or near the lake, one at a time.

Grandmother

Boy-Before

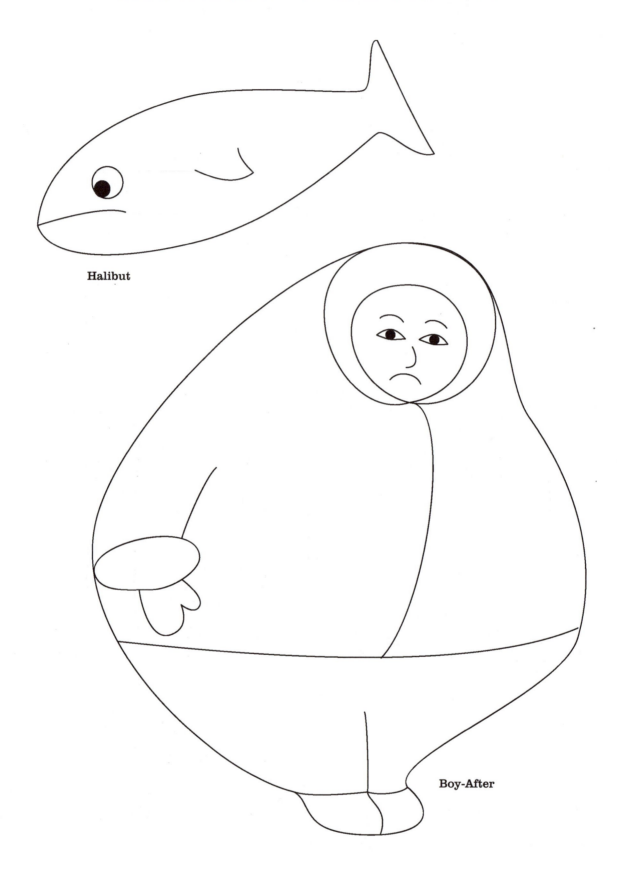

Halibut

Boy-After

THROUGH THE NEEDLE'S EYE
A Play for Readers' Theater

Six characters and a narrator

Boy	Fish	Walrus
Grandmother	Seal	Whale

NARRATOR: Once there was a boy who lived with his grandmother in a little house near the sea.

BOY: Grandma, I'm hungry!

GRANDMOTHER: Not again! You've eaten everything in the house.

BOY: But I'm still hungry.

GRANDMOTHER: Well, you'll just have to go out and hunt for something to eat.

NARRATOR: So the boy walked along the sea, and the first thing he found was a big fish.

BOY: This fish looks good. Guess I'll eat it.

FISH: Oh, please don't.

BOY: *Slurrrrp!*

NARRATOR: He ate it, scales and all. Then he saw a seal.

BOY: I'll eat this, too.

SEAL: You'll be sorry!

BOY: *Slurrrrp!*

NARRATOR: And he ate it, fur and all. Then he saw a walrus.

BOY: Mmmmmm.

WALRUS: You'll regret this.

BOY: *Slurrrrp!*

NARRATOR: He ate the walrus, tusks and all. Then he saw something really big. Something really, *really* big.

121

BOY: What a delicious-looking whale.

WHALE: I wouldn't do it if I were you.

BOY: *Slurrrrp!*

NARRATOR: Yes, he ate the whale, too. Blubber and all.

BOY: All this eating has made me thirsty. I wish I had something to drink. The ocean is too salty. Oh look! There's a lake. *Slurrrrp!*

NARRATOR: So he drank the lake, and then he walked back to his grandmother's house.

BOY: Grandma, I don't think I can get through the door. Mmmmm. Mmmmm.

GRANDMOTHER: Well, why don't you come in through the window.

BOY: (Trying) Mmmmm! Mmmmm! No, I can't get in that way, either.

GRANDMOTHER: Well, why don't you come in through the chimney.

BOY: (Trying) Mmmmm! Mmmmm! Mmmmm! No, I can't get in through the chimney, either.

GRANDMOTHER: Then you'll just have to come in through the eye of my needle.

NARRATOR: So the boy sque-e-e-ezed himself through the eye of his grandmother's needle and . . .

FISH, SEAL, WALRUS, AND WHALE: Ka-BOOM!

NARRATOR: . . . he exploded. Where that house had been, there was now a lake, and in the lake there were a fish, a seal, a walrus, and a whale swimming around and around. But no one ever saw that boy or his grandmother again.

14

BRER RABBIT'S RIDING HORSE
An African American Folktale

rer Rabbit is a favorite trickster in African American folktales. The plot of this story can be found in many other folktales of Africa and the Americas, and it is told with many different casts of characters. In Africa, for example, there is a tale about a frog who rides an elephant, and another about a hare who rides a hyena. In an Afro-Brazilian version, the Jabuti, the tortoise, tricks a leopard into letting him ride on his back like a horse.

It happened one time that Brer Rabbit and his old enemy Brer Wolf were courting the same young lady, Miss Molly Cottontail. One day, when Brer Rabbit went to the young lady's house, everybody there was talking about how strong and handsome Brer Wolf was. Naturally, Brer Rabbit got jealous.

"Brer Wolf? Brer Wolf?" Brer Rabbit sputtered. "Are we talking about that mangy old excuse for a dog? All of you should know that Brer Wolf is my riding horse. Yessir, I ride on his back whenever I please."

"Is that so?" said Molly Cottontail. "The next time Brer Wolf comes visiting, I'll tell him what you said about him."

Brer Rabbit went home in disgust, and it wasn't long before Brer Wolf came knocking at Brer Rabbit's door. Brer Rabbit lay down on his bed like he was sick and moaned, "Come in, Brer Wolf."

"Brer Rabbit," said Brer Wolf, "the folks down at Molly Cottontail's place told me that you said I am nothing but your riding horse. Now, that's a plain old lie, Brer Rabbit!"

"I have never in my life ridden you like a horse, Brer Wolf," said Brer Rabbit.

Well, Brer Wolf insisted that Brer Rabbit come with him to Molly Cottontail's and tell her in person that it was a lie.

"I'd like to do just that," said Brer Rabbit. "But as you can see, I'm feeling rather poorly. The doctor says I'm not strong enough to walk."

But Brer Wolf insisted, and so Brer Rabbit agreed to go if Brer Wolf would carry him.

"All right, then," said Brer Wolf. "Get up on my back and I'll carry you there."

Brer Rabbit looked at Brer Wolf. "Your back is so bony," he said. "I might get bruised sitting up there. Do you mind if I put a blanket on your back?"

"No, go ahead."

And so Brer Rabbit folded a blanket and put it on Brer Wolf's back. After he was finished, he climbed up. Brer Wolf began walking toward Molly Cottontail's. Suddenly, Brer Rabbit started to yell, "Oh dear! I think I'm going to fall off!"

Brer Wolf was angry. "Just hold on tight," he growled.

"I need something to hold on to, Brer Wolf," whined Brer Rabbit. "If you put the middle of this piece of rope between your teeth, I'll be able to hold one end in each paw."

So Brer Wolf held the middle of that piece of rope in his mouth. Brer Rabbit held one end in each paw. They went along toward Molly Cottontail's.

But after they had gone a ways, Brer Rabbit said, "Oh! Oh! Take me home, Brer Wolf, I can't go any farther."

"What's the matter now?" Brer Wolf growled.

"These flies and mosquitoes won't leave me alone," said Brer Rabbit.

So Brer Wolf cut a switch from a bush and gave it to Brer Rabbit. Brer Rabbit held the switch in his hand and hit it against Brer Wolf's ribs. Now they were almost at Molly Cottontail's. Molly and her folks were sitting on the front porch.

"Tell them, Brer Rabbit," whispered Brer Wolf. "Tell them I am not your riding horse."

But instead, Brer Rabbit hit Brer Wolf with the switch and shouted, "Gee-up, my horse, gee-up!" Those cottontails laughed till their wiskers curled, and Molly said, "Now I see, Brer Wolf, that you *are* Brer Rabbit's riding horse."

Brer Rabbit jumped down and hurried inside the house. Brer Wolf turned and ran away, and he never dared show his face at Molly's house again.

NOTES FOR FELTBOARD STORYTELLING

Make figures of Brer Rabbit, Brer Wolf, Molly Cottontail, Pa Cottontail, and Ma Cottontail. The figure of Brer Wolf must be colored on both sides, since he will need to face in both directions in order to first speak to Brer Rabbit and then carry him on his back. Use a piece of thin yarn to represent the rope that Brer Wolf holds in his mouth. Lift the wolf's head and pass the middle of the yarn underneath to keep it in place. Make Brer Rabbit's switch from a thin piece of felt and his saddle from a square of felt. A bed will represent Brer Rabbit's house, and you could also make a simple house or front porch for the Cottontails.

Molly Cottontail

Ma Cottontail

Brer Rabbit

Pa Cottontail

Brer Wolf

BRER RABBIT'S RIDING HORSE
A Play for Readers' Theater

Five characters and a narrator

Brer Rabbit   **Molly Cottontail**   **Pa Cottontail**

Brer Wolf   **Ma Cottontail**

NARRATOR: It happened one time that Brer Rabbit and his old enemy Brer Wolf were courting the same young lady, Miss Molly Cottontail. One day, when Brer Rabbit went to Molly's house, everybody there was talking about Brer Wolf.

PA COTTONTAIL: That Brer Wolf certainly is strong.

MA COTTONTAIL: Handsome, too.

PA COTTONTAIL: And he has such good manners. Any young lady would be happy to be Brer Wolf's girlfriend.

BREF RABBIT: Brer Wolf? Brer Wolf? Are you talking about that mangy old excuse for a dog? Why Brer Wolf is my riding horse. I ride on his back whenever I please.

MOLLY COTTONTAIL: Is that so? Next time Brer Wolf comes here, I'll just tell him what you said about him.

NARRATOR: Brer Rabbit went home in disgust. But it wasn't long before Brer Wolf came knocking at Brer Rabbit's door. Brer Rabbit quickly got into bed.

BRER WOLF: Brer Rabbit! Brer Rabbit! Let me in!

BRER RABBIT: (Weakly) Come in. Do come in, Brer Wolf.

BRER WOLF: Brer Rabbit, the folks down at Molly Cottontail's place told me that you said I am nothing but your riding horse. Now, that's a plain old lie, Brer Rabbit!

BRER RABBIT: I have never in my life ridden you like a horse, Brer Wolf.

BRER WOLF: Come with me to Molly Cottontail's and tell that to her, in person.

BRER RABBIT: I'd like to do that, Brer Wolf, because I want them to know the truth. But as you can see, I'm feeling rather poorly. The doctor says I'm not strong enough to walk.

BRER WOLF: I don't care, Brer Rabbit. I want you to come to Molly Cottontail's right now and tell them that I am not your riding horse.

128

Brer Rabbit: The only way I can get there is for you to carry me.

Brer Wolf: All right. Get up on my back, and I'll carry you there.

Brer Rabbit: Your back is bony, Brer Wolf. I might get bruised sitting up there. Do you mind if I put a blanket on your back?

Brer Wolf: No, go ahead.

Narrator: And so Brer Rabbit folded a blanket, put it on Brer Wolf's back, and climbed up. Brer Wolf began walking toward Molly Cottontail's.

Brer Rabbit: Stop, Brer Wolf! I think I'm going to fall off!

Brer Wolf: (Angrily) Just hold on tight.

Brer Rabbit: I need something to hold on to, Brer Wolf. Put this piece of rope between your teeth, and I'll hold one end in each paw.

Narrator: So Brer Wolf held the middle of that piece of rope in his mouth. Brer Rabbit held one end in each paw. They went along toward Molly Cottontail's.

Brer Rabbit: Oh! Oh! Take me home, Brer Wolf. I can't go any farther.

Brer Wolf: What's the matter now?

Brer Rabbit: These flies and mosquitoes won't leave me alone.

Brer Wolf: Calm down, Brer Rabbit. I'll just cut you a switch from this bush, and you can hit them with it.

Narrator: So Brer Rabbit held the switch in his paw. Now they were almost to Molly Cottontail's. Molly and all her family were sitting on the front porch.

Brer Wolf: (Softly) Tell them, Brer Rabbit. Tell them I am not your riding horse.

Narrator: But instead, Brer Rabbit hit Brer Wolf with the switch.

Brer Rabbit: (Shouting) Gee-up, my horse, gee-up!

Pa Cottontail and Ma Cottontail: Ha, ha, ha! Ha, ha, ha, ha! Ha, ha, ha!

Molly Cottontail: Now I see for myself, Brer Wolf, that you *are* Brer Rabbit's riding horse.

Narrator: Brer Rabbit jumped down and hurried inside the house. As for Brer Wolf, he turned and ran away, and he never dared show his face at Molly's house again.

15

THE BAD BEAR
An Anglo-American Folktale

This is an Appalachian version of a folktale known throughout the world. A monster with a voracious appetite swallows a whole slew of creatures. Fortunately for them, he doesn't chew before he swallows, and all are released alive at the end.

In an old log cabin in the mountains, there once lived a man and a woman and a little girl named Susie, and a little boy named Billy, and a pet monkey named Rags. Down the road a ways, in a hollow tree, lived a bad old, mean old bear.

One morning, the man and the woman sent Billy to the store to buy a chunk of meat. But earlier that day, the bear had gone to the store, grabbed that chunk of meat, and said, "I'm going to eat you, you fat chunk of meat." And he did! Swallowed it whole and never chewed it or anything. Then the bear went back to the hollow tree by the side of the road.

Along came Billy on his way to the store to get a chunk of meat, and the bear jumped out from the hollow tree. "Who are you?" asked Billy. "I'm the bad old bear with greasy, grimy hair. I ate a fat chunk of meat, and I'm a-gonna eat you, too!" And he did! Swallowed that little boy whole.

Well, when Billy didn't come home, the others became worried. The woman said to the little girl, "Why don't you go on down to the store and see what's keeping your brother so long"

Susie went out, and when she came to the hollow tree, out jumped that bad bear. "Who are you?" asked Susie. "I'm the bad old bear with greasy, grimy hair. I ate a fat chunk of meat and a little boy, and I'm a-gonna eat you, too!" And he did! Swallowed that little girl in one gulp.

The man and the woman were mighty concerned when Susie didn't come back, so the woman set out down the road to find out what had happened to them. When she came to the hollow tree, out jumped that bad bear. "Who are you?" asked the woman. "I'm the bad old bear with greasy, grimy hair. I ate a fat chunk of meat and a little boy and a little girl, and I'm a-gonna eat you, too!" And he did! Swallowed that woman down without chewing once.

Back home, the man and the monkey were scratching their heads, wondering what happened to the woman and Susie and Billy, so the man set out to find them. When he came to the hollow tree, out jumped that bad bear. "Who are you?" asked the man. "I'm the bad old bear with greasy, grimy hair. I ate a fat chunk of meat and a little boy and a little girl and a woman, and I'm a-gonna eat you, too!" And he did! Swallowed that man right there.

Well that monkey, Rags, went running all over the house, wondering why no one had come back. Finally, he set off down the road and came to the place where that bear was standing (he couldn't fit inside the hollow tree any more). And the monkey asked, "Who are you and why are you SO fat?" And the bear answered, "I'm the bad old bear with greasy, grimy hair. I ate a fat chunk of meat and a little boy and a little girl and a woman and a man, and I'm a-gonna eat you, too!"

Quick as anything, Rags climbed the tree, and the bear followed after him. But the bear stepped on a rotten branch and fell down to the ground and busted open.

The man said, "I'm out!"

The woman said, "I'm out!"

Susie said, "I'm out!"

Billy said, "I'm out!"

The fat chunk of meat said, "I'm out!"

And the monkey said, "I'm out, 'cause I was never in!"

Sure was a good thing that bear had such bad manners and swallowed them all whole, wasn't it?

NOTES FOR FELTBOARD STORYTELLING

Make figures of the bad bear, the father, the mother, Billy, Susie, and Rags, the monkey. Scenery includes the hollow tree and the house, which should both be made from felt so that figures of the characters will stick to them. Both should also be firmly attached to the feltboard with pins. Place the family members in front of the house and the bear in the middle of (inside) the hollow tree as the story begins. The incident of the bear eating the chunk of meat takes place "offstage"—remove the bear as you tell it. As the bear eats each character, remove that character quickly from the board and place it out of sight. All will reappear at the end of the tale.

House

The Bear's Hollow Tree

Bad Bear

Susie

Chunk of
Meat

Rags

Billy

Father

Mother

THE BAD BEAR
A Play for Readers' Theater

Seven characters and two narrators

Big Bad Bear   **Mother**   **Rags**

Fat Chunk of Meat   **Billy**

Father   **Susie**

NARRATOR 1: In an old log cabin in the mountains, there once lived a father, a mother, their daughter Susie, and their son Billy. They had a pet monkey named Rags.

NARRATOR 2: Down the road a piece, in a hollow tree, lived a bad old bear with greasy, grimy hair.

BEAR: Grrrr!

NARRATOR 1: One morning, the mother said—

MOTHER: Billy, won't you go on down to the store and buy us a chunk of meat?

BILLY: Sure, Mama.

NARRATOR 2: About that same time, the bear was thinking the same thing.

BEAR: I feel like going to the store and gettin' me a chunk of meat.

NARRATOR 1: So the bear went to the store, and he grabbed a chunk of meat without even paying for it.

BEAR: I'm a-gonna eat you, you fat chunk of meat!

NARRATOR 1: And he did! Swallowed it whole and never chewed it or anything. Then the bear went back to the hollow tree by the side of the road.

NARRATOR 2: Along came Billy on his way to the store to get a chunk of meat. When he passed by the hollow tree, the bear jumped out.

BEAR: Grrr!

BILLY: Who are you?

BEAR: I'm the bad old bear with greasy, grimy hair. I ate a fat chunk of meat, and I'm a-gonna eat you, too!

135

NARRATOR 1: And he did! Swallowed Billy whole.

NARRATOR 2: Well, when Billy didn't come home, the others became worried.

FATHER: I wonder what happened to Billy.

MOTHER: Susie, why don't you go on down to the store and see what's keeping your brother so long?

NARRATOR 1: Susie went out, and when she came to the hollow tree, out jumped that bear.

BEAR: Grrr!

SUSIE: Who are you?

BEAR: I'm the bad old bear with greasy, grimy hair. I ate a fat chunk of meat and a little boy, and I'm a-gonna eat you, too!

NARRATOR 1: And he did! Swallowed little Susie in one gulp.

NARRATOR 2: The father and mother were mighty concerned when Susie didn't come back, so the mother set out down the road to find out what had happened to them.

NARRATOR 1: When she came to the hollow tree, out jumped that bad bear.

BEAR: Grrr!

MOTHER: Who are you?

BEAR: I'm the bad old bear with greasy, grimy hair. I ate a fat chunk of meat and a little boy and a little girl, and I'm a-gonna eat you, too!

NARRATOR 2: And he did! Swallowed that woman down without chewing once.

NARRATOR 1: Back home, the father and the monkey were worrying something fierce about the mother, and Billy, and Susie, and so the father set out to find them.

NARRATOR 2: When he came to the hollow tree, out jumped that bad bear.

BEAR: Grrr!

FATHER: Who are you?

BEAR: I'm the bad old bear with greasy, grimy hair. I ate a fat chunk of meat and a little boy and a little girl and a woman, and I'm a-gonna eat you, too!

NARRATOR 1: And he did! Swallowed that man right there.

NARRATOR 2: Well, Rags, the monkey, was running all over the house, wondering why no one had come back. Finally, he set off down the road, and came to the bear.

NARRATOR 1: The bear was SO fat he couldn't fit inside the hollow tree.

BEAR: Grrr!

RAGS: Who are you, and why are you SO fat?

BEAR: I'm the bad old bear with greasy, grimy hair. I ate a fat chunk of meat and a little boy and a little girl and a woman and a man, and I'm a-gonna eat you, too!

NARRATOR 2: Quick as anything, Rags climbed the tree, and the bear followed after him.

NARRATOR 1: But the bear stepped on a rotten branch and fell down to the ground and busted open.

BEAR: Blam!

FATHER: Whew! I'm out!

MOTHER: I'm out!

SUSIE: I'm out!

BILLY: I'm out!

FAT CHUNK OF MEAT: I'm out!

RAGS: And I'm out, 'cause I was never in!

NARRATOR 2: It sure was a good thing that bear had such bad manners and swallowed them all whole, wasn't it?

16

JUAN AND THE GHOST
A Hispanic Folktale

People said Juan wasn't very smart, but then, only some-one who didn't think a lot was ever going to lay the ghost of the haunted house to rest. This is a New Mexi-can variant of a tale widely known in Europe, of a fear-less young man who spends a night in a haunted house.

Long ago, in a village in New Mexico, there stood an old house that everyone said was haunted. Children used to dare each other to spend the night there, but none of them was ever brave enough. Now, in this same village there lived a young man who, people said, had something missing upstairs. They made fun of him to his face and laughed at him behind his back. One day, a boy saw Juan walking along the road near the haunted house. "Juan! Amigo! I'll bet you couldn't spend the night in that old house."

"What's so hard about spending a night in that house?" asked Juan. "Sleeping is one of the things I do best. I'll sleep there tonight."

Juan went home; got a pot of soup, some kindling wood, and a blanket to keep himself warm. Then he set out for the haunted house. When it grew dark, Juan made a fire in the fireplace and hung his pot of soup on the hook.

Suddenly, a voice came from the chimney, "Can I fall? Can I fall?"

"Fall if you want to," Juan answered. "But don't fall in my soup!"

Down the chimney fell a ghostly leg. Juan looked at it, and stirred his soup.

The voice came from the chimney again, "Can I fall? Can I fall?"

"Fall if you want to," Juan answered. "But don't fall in my soup!"

Down the chimney fell a second leg. Juan looked at it, and stirred his soup.

The voice came from the chimney again, "Can I fall? Can I fall?"

"Fall if you want to," Juan answered. "But don't fall in my soup!"

Down the chimney fell a ghostly body. Juan looked at it, and stirred his soup a final time. As Juan began to eat his soup, the voice came again, "Can I fall? Can I fall?"

"Fall if you want to," Juan answered. "But don't fall in my soup!"

Down the chimney fell a ghostly arm. Juan looked at it, and ate his soup. Soon, another arm fell and, at last, a head. Then all the parts of that horrible body rose into the air and shook and danced themselves together. The ghost looked toward Juan from empty eye sockets.

"I was the owner of this house long ago," the ghost told him. "I lived an evil life and stole from people, and I had no one to bury my bones. If you will bury my bones, you may take my treasure, giving half to the church and keeping the other half for yourself."

The ghost led Juan outside to an old apple tree and told him to dig. Juan dug and dug until he found an old iron pot. The pot was full of gold coins. The old ghost's bones sank into the hole, and Juan covered them with dirt. The next morning, after a good night's sleep with the iron pot for a pillow, Juan carried half the gold coins to the church and the other half home. Afterwards, no one ever dared to call him just Juan. They called him *Señor* Juan, for he was the richest man in town.

NOTES FOR FELTBOARD STORYTELLING

Make two figures of Juan, one poorly dressed and one well-dressed. Also make the boy. Make the parts of the ghost separately. Set pieces are the small haunted house, which will be used as background in the opening scene, the fireplace, the apple tree, the pot of gold, and the dirt that covers first the pot of gold and later the ghost's bones.

The story is told in four scenes. For the first scene, use the haunted house, which should be placed near the top of the feltboard, and will seem to be in the distance. In the second scene, inside the house, the only scenery neces-

139

sary is the fireplace. As the parts of the ghost fall down the chimney, place them in a pile, later putting them together. Leave the ghost in place during the transition to the third scene, removing the fireplace and placing the apple tree, pot of gold, and dirt on top of it. When Juan buries the ghost, disassemble the bones and place them where the pot of gold had been. For the last scene, re-create the first scene exactly, except that Juan is now well-dressed.

Boy

Juan Rich

Juan Poor

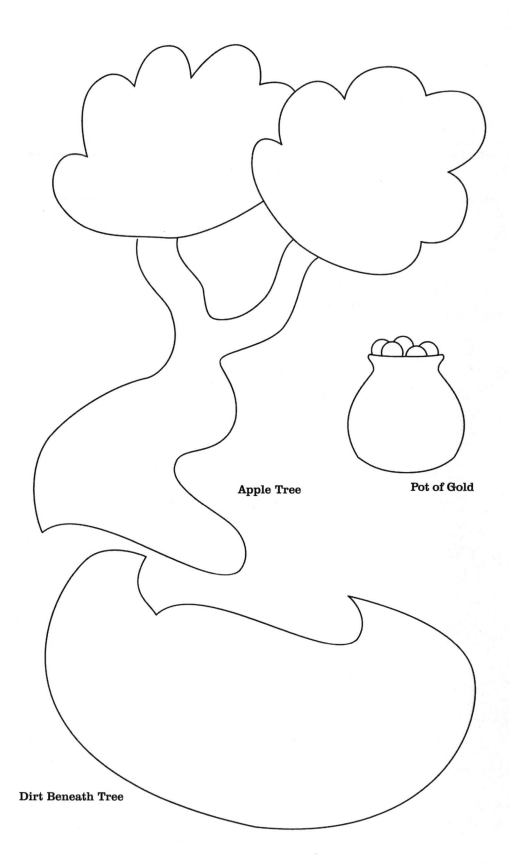

Apple Tree

Pot of Gold

Dirt Beneath Tree

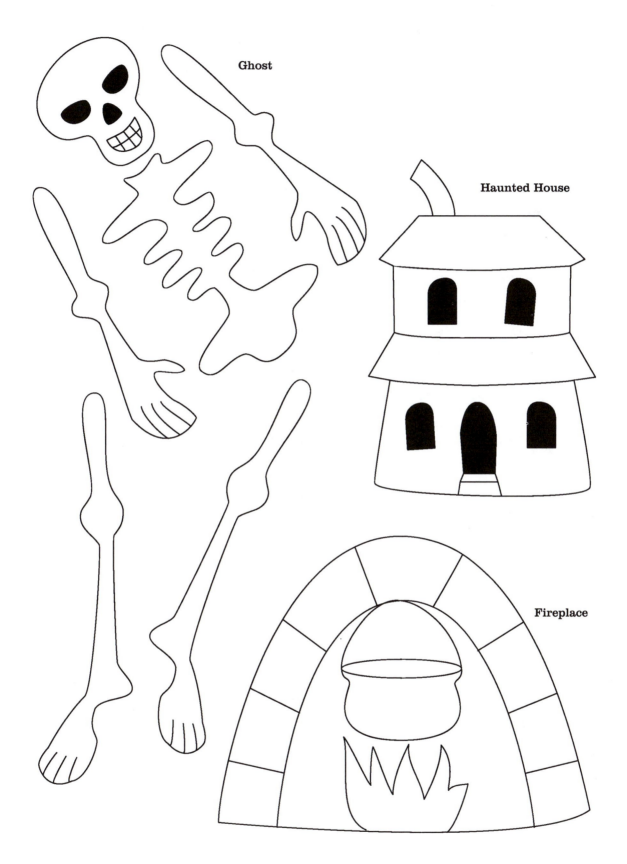

Ghost

Haunted House

Fireplace

JUAN AND THE GHOST
A Play for Readers' Theater

Three characters and three narrators

Boy

Juan

Ghost

NARRATOR 1: In a village in New Mexico, there once was an old house that everyone said was haunted. Children used to dare each other to spend the night there, but none of them was ever brave enough.

NARRATOR 2: In this same village, there lived a young man named Juan. People said he had something missing upstairs. He didn't act like other people, and so they made fun of him.

NARRATOR 3: One day, a boy saw Juan walking along the road near the haunted house.

BOY: Hola, Juan. Don't you think it's a shame that no one in town is brave enough to spend a night in the old abandoned house? Imagine! A whole village full of cowards.

JUAN: What's so hard about spending a night in that house?

BOY: Could you do it?

JUAN: Sleeping is one of the things I do best. I'll sleep there tonight.

NARRATOR 1: Juan went home and got a pot of soup and some kindling wood and set out for the haunted house.

NARRATOR 2: When it grew dark, Juan made a fire in the fireplace and hung his pot of soup on the hook.

NARRATOR 3: Suddenly, a voice came from the chimney.

GHOST: Can I fall? Can I fall?

JUAN: Fall if you want to. But don't fall in my soup.

NARRATOR 1: Down the chimney fell a ghostly leg. Juan looked at it, and stirred his soup.

GHOST: Can I fall? Can I fall?

JUAN: Fall if you want to. But don't fall in my soup.

NARRATOR 2: Down the chimney fell a second ghostly leg. Juan looked at it, and stirred his soup.

GHOST: Can I fall? Can I fall?

JUAN: Fall if you want to. But don't fall in my soup.

NARRATOR 3: Down the chimney fell a ghostly body. Juan looked at it, and stirred his soup a final time. As Juan began to eat his soup, the voice came again.

GHOST: Can I fall? Can I fall?

JUAN: Fall if you want to. But don't fall in my soup.

NARRATOR 1: Down the chimney fell a ghostly arm. Juan looked at it, and ate his soup.

NARRATOR 2: Soon another ghostly arm fell, and, at last, a ghostly head. Then all the parts of that ghostly body rose into the air and shook and danced themselves together.

NARRATOR 3: The ghost looked at Juan from empty eye sockets.

GHOST: I was the owner of this house long ago, and I lived an evil life, stealing from people. No one wanted to bury my bones. If you will bury my bones, you may take my treasure. Give half to the church, and keep the other half for yourself.

NARRATOR 1: The ghost led Juan outside to an old apple tree and told him to dig.

NARRATOR 2: Juan dug and dug until he found an old iron pot, which was full of gold coins.

NARRATOR 3: The old ghost's bones sank into the hole, and Juan covered them with dirt.

GHOST: Thank y-o-o-o-u.

NARRATOR 1: Juan carried half the gold coins to the church and the other half to his house.

NARRATOR 2: Afterwards, people stopped making fun of him . . .

NARRATOR 3: . . . because he was the richest man in town.

BOY: Buenos días, *Señor* Juan!

JUAN: Buenos días. And thank you for telling me I should spend the night in the haunted house.

145

17

THE RABBIT WHO WANTED RED WINGS
An Anglo-American Folktale

With its message, "You're perfect just the way you are," this story has long been a favorite of young children.

Once there was a little rabbit who had two beautiful long pink ears and two bright red eyes and four soft little feet. But that little rabbit was not happy at all. He wanted to be like somebody else instead of the nice little rabbit that he was.

When the grey squirrel rushed by, the little rabbit would say to his mother, "I wish I had a big, bushy tail like the squirrel. And when the yellow duck waddled by, the little rabbit would say to his mother, "I wish I had pretty webbed feet like the yellow duck."

The little rabbit went on wishing until his mother was tired of listening to him. One day, the old groundhog heard him and said, "Why don't you go down to the wishing pond. Look at yourself in the water, turn around three times, and you'll get your wish." So the little rabbit hopped along, all alone, through the woods until he came to a pool of green water lying in the hollow of a tree stump. That was the wishing pond. Sitting there, just on the edge of the wishing pond, was a red bird getting ready to take a drink. When the little rabbit saw the bird, he made his wish. "I wish I had a pair of wings like that red bird." The rabbit hopped up onto the tree stump. He looked at himself in the water, he turned around three times, and then his back began to feel scratchy. Out of his soft fur grew a pair of red wings.

Then the little rabbit flapped his wings and tried and tried to fly. "It must take lots of practice," he said, "or else wings don't work very well on a rabbit." He tried and tried to fly until he was very tired. He decided to go home and rest.

The little rabbit hopped home to his rabbit hole. "Mama! Look at me," he cried.

"Who are you?" his mother asked.

"I'm your little rabbit!"

"No, my little rabbit does not have red wings." And his mother would not let him come inside.

The little rabbit went to the grey squirrel's home and asked, "May I sleep here tonight?"

"I've never seen a rabbit with red wings before," said the grey squirrel. "You cannot sleep here."

The little rabbit hopped down to the duck's nest and asked if he could spend the night there.

"I have never seen you before," said the little yellow duck. "You can't sleep here."

So, finally, the little rabbit came to the old groundhog's den, and the old groundhog knew he was the little rabbit and let him sleep there. But the groundhog's den was full of broken twigs and stones, and the little rabbit did not sleep very well.

The next morning the little rabbit told the old groundhog that he didn't want the red wings after all, because now no one knew who he was.

"Why don't you go to the wishing pond again and wish the wings off," suggested the groundhog. So the little rabbit went back to the wishing pond. He looked at himself in the water and said, "I want to be just my plain old self again." He turned around three times, and the wings were gone.

He went back home and knocked at the door of the rabbit hole, and his mother hugged him tight. "There you are, my beautiful little rabbit," she said. "Come in and sit with me. I love you. You are perfect just the way you are."

NOTES FOR FELTBOARD STORYTELLING

Make figures of the little rabbit, the mother rabbit, the grey squirrel, the yellow duck, the groundhog, the red bird, and the wishing pond in the tree stump. Make four doors to represent the houses of the mother rabbit, grey squirrel, yellow duck, and groundhog. To make the rabbit sprout red wings, you have two choices. Either make separate wings, and be sure to hold them onto the rabbit figure as you move it, or make a duplicate little rabbit with red wings, and substitute it for the first rabbit at the proper point in the story.

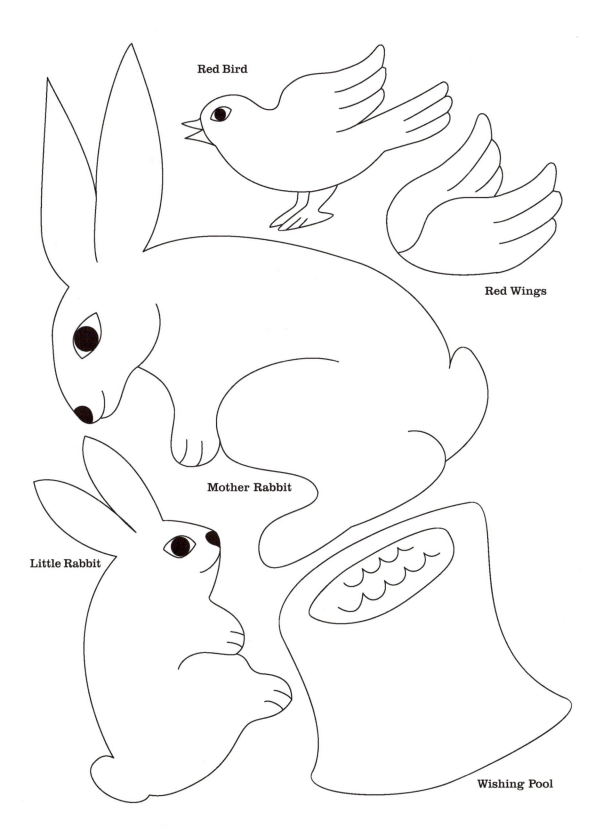

Red Bird

Red Wings

Mother Rabbit

Little Rabbit

Wishing Pool

Yellow Duck

Grey Squirrel

Groundhog

THE RABBIT WHO WANTED RED WINGS
A Play for Readers' Theater

Five characters and one narrator

Little Rabbit   **Grey Squirrel**   **Groundhog**

Mother Rabbit   **Yellow Duck**

NARRATOR: Once there was a little rabbit who had two beautiful long pink ears, two bright red eyes, and four soft little feet. But that rabbit was not happy. He wanted to be like somebody else instead of the nice little rabbit that he was.

MOTHER RABBIT: Good morning, my beautiful little rabbit.

LITTLE RABBIT: Good morning, mother. Good morning, grey squirrel.

GREY SQUIRREL: Good morning, little rabbit.

LITTLE RABBIT: You have a nice bushy tail.

GREY SQUIRREL: Thank you, little rabbit.

LITTLE RABBIT: Mama, I wish I had a bushy tail.

MOTHER RABBIT: You have a nice white fluffy tail.

LITTLE RABBIT: Good morning, yellow duck.

YELLOW DUCK: Good morning, little rabbit.

LITTLE RABBIT: You have pretty webbed feet.

YELLOW DUCK: Thank you, little rabbit.

LITTLE RABBIT: Mama, I wish I had webbed feet.

MOTHER RABBIT: You have four nice soft little feet.

LITTLE RABBIT: I wish I had . . .

MOTHER RABBIT: (Interrupting) Your wishing makes me tired. Please go outside and play.

LITTLE RABBIT: I wish I had a bushy tail. I wish I had webbed feet. I wish I had . . .

GROUNDHOG: (Interrupting) Hello, little rabbit.

151

LITTLE RABBIT: Hello, groundhog.

GROUNDHOG: Rabbit, are you wishing to be different?

LITTLE RABBIT: Yes.

GROUNDHOG: Why don't you go down to the wishing pond.

LITTLE RABBIT: What should I do there?

GROUNDHOG: Look at yourself in the water.

LITTLE RABBIT: Then what?

GROUNDHOG: Turn around three times.

LITTLE RABBIT: Then what?

GROUNDHOG: Make a wish and it will come true.

LITTLE RABBIT: I'll go there right now.

NARRATOR: The rabbit went to the wishing pond, and there he saw a little bird with red wings. The rabbit looked into the pond and turned around three times.

LITTLE RABBIT: I wish, I wish, I wish. I wish I had red wings. I do! I do have red wings! Now I can fly.

NARRATOR: The little rabbit flapped his wings over and over, but he could not fly.

LITTLE RABBIT: Maybe wings don't work on a rabbit. Oh well, I'm tired. I want to go to sleep.

NARRATOR: The little rabbit hopped back home and knocked on the door.

LITTLE RABBIT: Mama, can I come in and go to sleep?

MOTHER RABBIT: Who are you?

LITTLE RABBIT: I'm your little rabbit.

MOTHER RABBIT: No, my little rabbit doesn't have red wings.

NARRATOR: And the little rabbit's mother closed the door. So the little rabbit went to the grey squirrel's house and knocked on the door.

LITTLE RABBIT: May I sleep in your house?

GREY SQUIRREL: Who are you? I've never seen a rabbit with red wings before.

NARRATOR: And the grey squirrel wouldn't let him in. So the little rabbit went to the yellow duck's house and knocked at the door.

LITTLE RABBIT: May I sleep in your house?

YELLOW DUCK: Who are you? I've never seen a rabbit with red wings before.

NARRATOR: And the yellow duck wouldn't let him sleep there, either. So the little rabbit went to the groundhog's house and knocked on the door.

LITTLE RABBIT: May I sleep in your house?

GROUNDHOG: Yes, little rabbit with red wings. You may sleep on the floor in my house.

NARRATOR: The little rabbit lay down on the floor, but he couldn't sleep because the groundhog's den was full of sticks and rocks.

LITTLE RABBIT: Ouch! Ouch! I can't sleep. The sticks and rocks hurt me.

NARRATOR: The next morning, the little rabbit was sad.

LITTLE RABBIT: I don't want these red wings. These wings are terrible!

GROUNDHOG: Why don't you go to the wishing pond and wish yourself back to the way you were.

LITTLE RABBIT: I will! I will! Goodbye.

NARRATOR: The little rabbit hopped to the wishing pond. He looked into the pond and turned around three times.

LITTLE RABBIT: I wish, I wish, I wish. I wish I was my regular self again!

NARRATOR: The wings disappeared. The little rabbit hopped home again and knocked on the door.

LITTLE RABBIT: Mama, may I come in and rest?

MOTHER RABBIT: There you are my beautiful little rabbit with a nice white tail and four soft little feet. Come in and sit with me. I love you. You are perfect just the way you are.

18

THE MOUSE AND THE COAL
A French-Canadian Folktale

The little mouse is very, very naughty, and as a result she loses her tail. Then she must run all over the place and arrange a series of trades in order to get the tailor to sew on her tail. This tale may seem silly at first, but it teaches how a simple task can become complicated, and how one must persevere to get what one wants.

Once there was a little mouse that lived in a little house, and she made friends with a little lump of coal that was burning in the fireplace. The two of them went for a walk, and they came to a stream. The mouse wanted to cross the stream, but the coal said, "How can we cross the stream? There isn't a bridge."

"That's no problem," said the mouse. "I'll put a piece of straw across, and we'll walk on it."

"You must be crazy!" said the coal. "I would catch the straw on fire, and then the straw would burn, and I would fall into the stream and drown."

"No, you're the crazy one," the mouse told him. "How could you set the straw on fire if the straw is on the water? The water would put out the fire right away."

So the mouse found a piece of straw and laid it across the stream. The little coal still didn't want to cross, but finally he agreed. When he was halfway across, the straw began to smoke and burn. The straw broke, and the lump of coal fell into the stream and drowned.

Then that bad mouse started to laugh. She laughed and laughed and laughed so hard that her tail fell off.

"Oh, poor me!" the mouse cried. "I'm being punished for laughing at my friend. What shall I do? Oh, I know. I'll go see the tailor, and he will sew my tail back on."

The mouse walked and walked until she came to the tailor's shop and said,

> Kind tailor, good tailor,
> Please sew my tail back on.

"I would gladly help you," the tailor said, "but I have no thread. Go ask the pig to give you some."

So the mouse walked and walked until she came to the pig's house, and she said,

> Good pig, nice pig,
> Please give me some thread,
> So that the tailor can sew my tail back on.

"You want my thread," the pig said, "but I have nothing to eat. Go to the miller and get me some grain. Then I will give you some thread."

So the mouse walked and walked until she came to the mill, and she said,

> Good miller, generous miller,
> Please give me some grain,
> So that I may give grain to the pig,
> So that the pig will give me thread,
> So that I may give the tailor thread,
> So that he will sew my tail back on for me.

But the miller answered, "I am too poor to give anything away. But if you bring me some milk from the cow, you may have some grain."

So the mouse walked and walked until she came to the cow, and she said,

> Good cow, sweet cow,
> Please give me some milk,
> So that I may give the milk to the miller,
> So that the miller will give me grain,
> So that I may give grain to the pig,
> So that the pig will give me thread,
> So that I may give the tailor thread,
> So that he will sew my tail back on for me.

"I would gladly give you milk," said the cow, "but I am so thirsty. Bring me a drink of water."

So the mouse went to the stream and said,

> Oh wicked stream, who swallowed my friend, the lump of coal,
> Please give me some water,
> So that I may give the cow water,
> So that the cow will give me milk,
> So that I may give the milk to the miller,
> So that the miller will give me grain,
> So that I may give grain to the pig,
> So that the pig will give me thread,
> So that I may give the tailor thread,
> So that he will sew my tail back on for me.

"Very well," said the stream, "it's the least I can do."

> And so the stream gave the mouse water,
> And the mouse took water to the cow,
> And the cow gave the mouse milk,
> And the mouse carried the milk to the miller,
> And the miller gave the mouse grain,
> And the mouse carried the grain to the pig,
> And the pig gave the mouse thread,
> And the mouse gave the thread to the tailor,
> And the tailor sewed the mouse's tail back on,
> And the mouse promised never to laugh at another's
>   misfortune again.

NOTES FOR FELTBOARD STORYTELLING

Make figures of the mouse, the mouse's tail, the coal, the straw, the tailor, the pig, the miller, the cow, and the stream. Place the mouse and her tail, as if it were attached to her body, near the center of the feltboard before the children see it. Then, as the story progresses, place the other figures and scenery around her (until her tail falls off, she doesn't move). The items that are given to the mouse do not need to be represented on the feltboard. Children will see them in their imaginations.

Mouse

Tail

Coal

Pig

Stream

Cow

Straw

Miller

Tailor

THE MOUSE AND THE COAL
A Play for Readers' Theater

Seven characters and one narrator

Mouse	Pig	Stream
Coal	Miller	
Tailor	Cow	

NARRATOR: Once there was a little mouse that lived in a little house, and she made friends with a little lump of coal that burned in the fireplace. The two of them went out for a walk, and they came to a stream.

MOUSE: Let's cross this stream.

COAL: How can we get across? There isn't a bridge.

MOUSE: That's no problem. I'll put a piece of straw across, and we'll walk on it.

COAL: You must be crazy! I would catch the straw on fire, and then the straw would burn, and I would fall into the stream and drown.

MOUSE: You're the crazy one. The water would put out the fire right away.

COAL: No, I still don't want to walk across on a straw.

MOUSE: Come on, scaredy cat.

COAL: Oh, all right.

NARRATOR: So the mouse found a piece of straw and laid it across the stream. Then she pushed the coal ahead of her.

MOUSE: Bon voyage!

COAL: Oh! Oh! Oh! I smell smoke!

NARRATOR: The coal caught the straw on fire, and the straw broke, and the lump of coal fell into the stream and drowned.

COAL: Aaaaaah!

NARRATOR: The mouse laughed . . .

MOUSE: Hee, hee, hee . . .

NARRATOR: . . . and laughed so hard . . .

160

MOUSE: . . . ha, ha, ha . . .

NARRATOR: . . . that her tail fell off!

MOUSE: Oh no! Oh, poor me! I'm being punished for laughing at my friend. What shall I do? Oh, I know. I'll go see the tailor, and he will sew my tail back on for me.

NARRATOR: The mouse walked and walked until she came to the tailor's shop.

MOUSE: Kind tailor, good tailor,
Please sew my tail back on.

TAILOR: I would gladly do that, but I have no thread. Go ask the pig to give you some.

NARRATOR: So the mouse walked and walked until she came to the pig's house.

MOUSE: Good pig, nice pig,
Please give me some thread,
So that the tailor will sew my tail back on.

PIG: You want my thread, but I have nothing to eat. Go to the miller and get me some grain. Then I will give you some thread.

NARRATOR: So the mouse walked and walked until she came to the mill.

MOUSE: Good miller, generous miller,
Please give me some grain,
So that I may give grain to the pig,
So that the pig will give me thread,
So that I may give the tailor thread,
So that the tailor will sew my tail back on for me.

MILLER: I am too poor to give anything away. But if you bring me some milk from the cow, you may have some grain.

NARRATOR: So the mouse walked and walked until she came to the cow.

MOUSE: Good cow, sweet cow,
Please give me some milk,
So that I may give the milk to the miller,
So that the miller will give me grain,
So that I may give grain to the pig,
So that the pig will give me thread,
So that I may give the tailor thread,
So that the tailor will sew my tail back on for me.

Cow: I would gladly give you milk, but I am so thirsty. Bring me a drink of water.

Narrator: So the mouse went to the stream.

Mouse: Oh wicked stream, who swallowed my friend, the lump of coal,
      Please give me some water,
      So that I may give the cow water,
      So that the cow will give me milk,
      So that I may give the milk to the miller,
      So that the miller will give me grain,
      So that I may give grain to the pig,
      So that the pig will give me thread,
      So that I may give the tailor thread,
      So that the tailor will sew my tail back on for me.

Stream: Very well. It's the least I can do.

Narrator: And so the stream gave the mouse water.

Mouse: And I took water to the cow.

Cow: And I gave the mouse milk.

Mouse: And I carried the milk to the miller.

Miller: And I gave the mouse grain.

Mouse: And I carried the grain to the pig.

Pig: And I gave the mouse thread.

Mouse: And I gave the thread to the tailor.

Tailor: And I sewed the mouse's tail back on.

Mouse: And I promised never to laugh at someone else's misfortune again.

19

THE TALKATIVE TORTOISE
A Guatemalan Folktale

The earliest known version of this tale was recorded in India two thousand years ago. The tale is also known in the oral traditions of Asia, Africa, Europe, and the Americas. In most of these tales, the tortoise is merely too chatty; in this Guatemalan variant, however, he is downright mean, and thus really deserves his fall from the sky.

There once was a tortoise who just couldn't keep his mouth shut. It wasn't that he talked a lot; it was just that when he did talk, he usually had something mean to say about someone. The tortoise was always making fun of other animals, and therefore, had scarcely any friends at all. Just about the only animal that would talk to him was the buzzard. One afternoon, the tortoise sat on the ground and watched the buzzard take off and fly up into the sky. The buzzard just circled on the wind currents for hours and hours.

"That buzzard can see everything for miles around," said the tortoise. "I wish I could fly."

Just then, the buzzard landed on the ground beside the tortoise.

"It sure must be nice to see the world from high up in the air," said the tortoise.

"Yes, it is," the buzzard told him. "It's too bad you can't fly, my friend. But each of us must be happy with the gifts we are given."

"Could you give me a ride on your back and take me up with you?" asked the tortoise. "Oh, you're probably not strong enough. You're probably not a good enough flier."

"You're so small and insignificant," said the buzzard. "You would be no more trouble to carry than a flea."

And the buzzard flapped down to the ground. Slowly, the tortoise climbed onto his friend's back. The buzzard flapped his wings and took off, while the tortoise hung on with all four feet. Soon they were circling on the wind currents.

"How wonderful!" cried the tortoise. "I can fly!"

The tortoise settled back to enjoy the ride and the view. But soon he began to smell something. Something terrible. It was the buzzard's breath.

"Say, friend," said the tortoise. "I smell something bad. It smells like dead, rotten things. Have you been eating dead, rotten things?"

"Of course," the buzzard replied. "That's what buzzards eat. Dead, rotten things. You don't mind, do you?"

The tortoise looked down at the ground. It was far, far away. "Oh, no. I don't mind," he said.

But the tortoise just couldn't keep his mouth shut. He tried not to say anything else, but at last he just couldn't help himself.

"Buzzard?"

"Yes?"

"Buzzard?"

"Yes?"

"Buzzard, you *stink!*"

The buzzard went into a nose dive. Down, down, down fell the tortoise, and he landed on his back on the hard, hard ground.

It took him nearly a week to find someone who would agree to turn him over on his feet again. He wasn't hurt, but his shell was cracked. You can still see those cracks today on the tortoise's back. And you'll notice that the tortoise has learned his lesson. Now, he never says a single word!

NOTES FOR FELTBOARD STORYTELLING

Though scenery is not absolutely necessary for telling this tale, you could make a bush to represent the ground and a cloud to place beneath the flying buzzard. Make the figure of the tortoise two-sided. On the first side, his shell should have no cracks. On the second side, the lines should be clearly visible to the audience. In addition, make two figures of the buzzard, one sitting, and one flying.

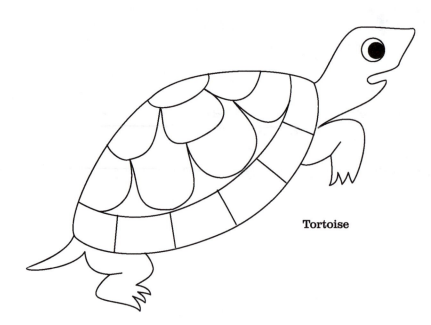

Tortoise

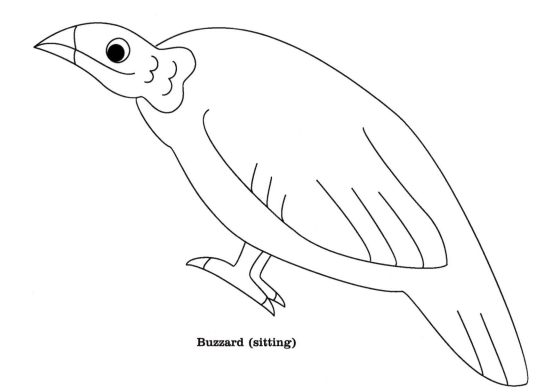

Buzzard (sitting)

Buzzard (flying)

THE TALKATIVE TORTOISE
A Play for Readers' Theater

Two characters and one narrator

Tortoise

Buzzard

NARRATOR: There once was a tortoise who just couldn't keep his mouth shut. He usually had something mean to say about someone.

TORTOISE: You're not a very good narrator.

NARRATOR: As I was saying, the tortoise always made jokes about the way other animals looked or copied their voices in a nasty way.

TORTOISE: (Nastily) . . . or copied their voices in a nasty way.

NARRATOR: The fact is, the tortoise had scarcely any friends at all. Just about the only animal that would talk to him was the buzzard. One afternoon, the tortoise sat on the ground and watched the buzzard take off and fly up into the sky. The buzzard just circled on the wind currents for hours and hours.

TORTOISE: That buzzard can see everything for miles around. I wish I could fly.

NARRATOR: Soon, the buzzard landed on the ground next to the tortoise.

TORTOISE: It sure must be nice to see the world from high up in the air.

BUZZARD: Yes, it is. It's too bad you can't fly, my friend. But each of us must be happy with the gifts we are given.

TORTOISE: I don't suppose you could give me a ride on your back and take me up with you. You're probably not strong enough. You're probably not a good enough flier.

BUZZARD: You're so small and insignificant. You would be no more trouble to carry than a flea.

TORTOISE: (To himself) I could tell him how many fleas I see on his back right now, but I'd better keep my mouth shut if I want him to give me a ride. (To the buzzard) You are right. I am small and insignificant. You probably won't even know I am on your back. We can sail around for hours.

BUZZARD: Well, I guess I will take you for a ride.

168

NARRATOR: The tortoise climbed slowly onto his friend's back and settled between his wings.

TORTOISE: Be careful, now. Don't let me fall.

NARRATOR: The buzzard flapped his wings and took off, while the tortoise hung on with all four feet. Soon, they were circling on the wind currents.

TORTOISE: How wonderful! I can fly!

BUZZARD: Didn't you forget to say, "with the buzzard's help?"

TORTOISE: Excuse me. With your help, of course.

NARRATOR: The tortoise settled back to enjoy the ride and the view. But soon, he began to smell something. He smelled the buzzard's breath.

TORTOISE: Say, friend, I smell something bad. It smells like dead, rotten things. Have you been eating dead, rotten things?

BUZZARD: Of course. That's what we buzzards eat. Dead, rotten things. You don't mind, do you?

TORTOISE: Oh no, not at all.

NARRATOR: Looking down and noticing that the ground was a long way off, the tortoise tried to keep his mouth shut. He tried not to say anything else, but, at last, he just couldn't help himself.

TORTOISE: Buzzard?

BUZZARD: Yes?

TORTOISE: Buzzard?

BUZZARD: Yes?

TORTOISE: Buzzard, you *stink!*

NARRATOR: The buzzard went into a nose dive.

BUZZARD: (Making a noise like an airplane) Nye-e-e-er!

NARRATOR: Down, down, down fell the tortoise.

TORTOISE: Aaaaaaah!

NARRATOR: He landed on his back on the hard, hard ground.

169

TORTOISE: Yowch!

NARRATOR: It took him nearly a week to find someone who would agree to turn him over on his feet again.

TORTOISE: Excuse me, narrator. Would you mind turning me over?

NARRATOR: After all those terrible things you said about me?

TORTOISE: I didn't mean them.

NARRATOR: Stay on your back and think about it for a while. As I was saying, the tortoise wasn't hurt, but his shell was cracked. You can still see those cracks today on the tortoise's back. And you'll notice that the tortoise has learned his lesson. Now, he never says a single word.

20

THE TWO MONKEYS
A Cuban Folktale

Chain tales like this one exist in the folklore of many countries. Compare this Cuban tale to "The Bird and Her Babies" from India and the Irish folktale, "Munachar and Manachar," both in this book. A chain tale features a character who needs to get something done and who asks a series of people, animals, and even objects to help, setting up a humorous chain reaction. Notice that the character who finally agrees to help the monkey is the one who is promised something valuable in return.

Once upon a time, a little monkey was swinging through the trees when she saw a garbanzo bean on the jungle floor. She dropped to the ground and picked it up. The monkey couldn't decide whether to eat the bean right away or plant it and grow a garbanzo bean plant for later. While she was thinking, a bigger monkey spied the garbanzo bean in her hand. The big monkey swung down from the trees and grabbed it.

"Give me back my garbanzo bean!" the little monkey demanded, but the big monkey refused. So the little monkey went to see the king, and said,

Sire, put that big monkey in jail.
The big monkey took my garbanzo bean and won't give it back.

But the king said, "I'm sorry, little monkey, but a garbanzo bean is no big deal." So the little monkey went along and went along until she met a rat, and said,

Rat, eat the king's robe.
The king won't put the big monkey in jail.
The big monkey took my garbanzo bean and won't give it back.

But the rat said, "No, little monkey. If I eat the king's robe, I'll be in big trouble." So the little monkey went along and went along until she met a cat, and said,

Cat, catch that rat.
The rat won't eat the king's robe.
The king won't put the big monkey in jail.
The big monkey took my garbanzo bean and won't give it back.

But the cat said, "Sorry, little monkey, I'm just too tired right now." So the little monkey went along and went along until she came to a stick, and said.

Stick, scratch that cat.
The cat won't catch the rat.
The rat won't eat the king's robe.
The king won't put the big monkey in jail.
The big monkey took my garbanzo bean and won't give it back.

But the stick said, "Sorry, little monkey, but that's just too much trouble." So the little monkey went along and went along until she met a candle, and said.

Candle, burn that stick.
The stick won't scratch the cat.
The cat won't catch the rat.
The rat won't eat the king's robe.
The king won't put the big monkey in jail.
The big monkey took my garbanzo bean and won't give it back.

But the candle said, "I'm too busy, little monkey. Come back later." So the little monkey went along and went along until she met some water, and said.

Water, put out that candle.
The candle won't burn the stick.
The stick won't scratch the cat.
The cat won't catch the rat.
The rat won't eat the king's robe.

The king won't put the big monkey in jail.
The big monkey took my garbanzo bean and won't give it back.

But the water said, "No, little monkey. The candle's smoke might get me dirty."
So the little monkey went along and went along until she met a dog, and said,

Dog, drink that water.
The water won't put out the candle.
The candle won't burn the stick.
The stick won't scratch the cat.
The cat won't catch the rat.
The rat won't eat the king's robe.
The king won't put the big monkey in jail.
The big monkey took my garbanzo bean and won't give it back.

But the dog said, "Sorry, little monkey. I'm not thirsty right now." So the little monkey went along and went along until she met an ant, and said,

Ant, bite that dog.
The dog won't drink the water.
The water won't put out the candle.
The candle won't burn the stick.
The stick won't scratch the cat.
The cat won't catch the rat.
The rat won't eat the king's robe.
The king won't put the big monkey in jail.
The big monkey took my garbanzo bean and won't give it back.

And the ant said, "What will you give me if I do?" "I'll share the garbanzo bean with you," said the little monkey.

Then the ant began to bite the dog.
The dog began to drink the water.
The water began to put out the candle.
The candle began to burn the stick.
The stick began to scratch the cat.
The cat began to catch the rat.
The rat began to eat the king's robe.
And the king began to put the big monkey in jail.
And the big monkey gave the little monkey her garbanzo bean.

"Little ant," said the little monkey, "do you want to eat the garbanzo bean now or plant it in the ground for later?"
"Let's plant it," said the ant. "That way we'll have more next year."
And they did.

NOTES FOR FELTBOARD STORYTELLING

Make figures of the little monkey, the big monkey, the king, the rat, the cat, the stick, the candle, the water, the dog, and the ant. Cut a small circle of yellow or beige felt to represent the garbanzo bean. You might also want to make a garbanzo bean plant with lots of beans on it and place it on the board at the very end of the story.

This is a simple story to tell on the feltboard. Place the figures in a circular pattern as they appear, then remove each one as it takes its part in the final chain reaction. The ant and the little monkey are the only ones left at the end.

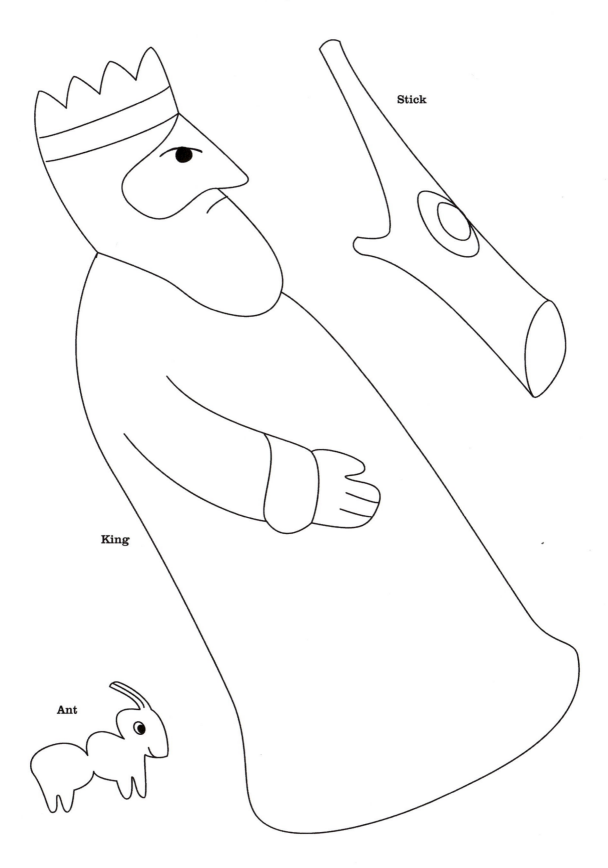

Stick

King

Ant

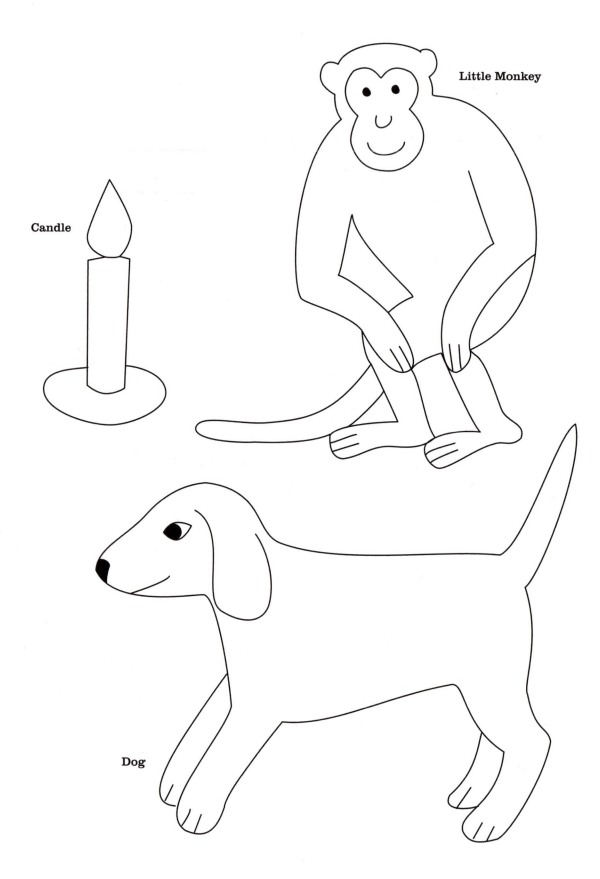

Candle

Little Monkey

Dog

Water

Big Monkey

Rat

Cat

177

THE TWO MONKEYS
A Play for Readers' Theater

Ten characters and one narrator

Little Monkey	**Cat**	**Water**
Big Monkey	**Stick**	**Dog**
King	**Candle**	**Ant**
Rat		

NARRATOR: Once upon a time, a little monkey was swinging through the trees when he saw a garbanzo bean on the jungle floor. He dropped to the ground and picked it up.

LITTLE MONKEY: Chee, chee, chee! A garbanzo bean! Should I eat it right now, or should I plant it in the ground for later?

NARRATOR: The little monkey couldn't decide. While she was thinking about it, a big monkey spied the garbanzo bean in her hand. The big monkey swung down from the trees, and grabbed it.

BIG MONKEY: Chee, chee, cheeee! A garbanzo bean!

LITTLE MONKEY: Give me back my garbanzo bean!

BIG MONKEY: No.

NARRATOR: So the little monkey went to see the king.

LITTLE MONKEY: Sire, put the big monkey in jail.
The big monkey took my garbanzo bean and won't give it back.

KING: I'm sorry, little monkey, but a garbanzo bean is no big deal.

NARRATOR: So the little monkey went along and went along until she met a rat.

LITTLE MONKEY: Rat, eat the king's robe.
The king won't put the big monkey in jail.
The big monkey took my garbanzo bean and won't give it back.

RAT: No, little monkey. If I eat the king's robe, I'll be in big trouble.

NARRATOR: So the little monkey went along and went along until she met a cat.

178

LITTLE MONKEY: Cat, catch the rat.
The rat won't eat the king's robe.
The king won't put the big monkey in jail.
The big monkey took my garbanzo bean and won't give it back.

CAT: Sorry, little monkey, I'm just too tired right now.

NARRATOR: So the little monkey went along and went along until she came to a stick.

LITTLE MONKEY: Stick, scratch the cat.
The cat won't catch the rat.
The rat won't eat the king's robe.
The king won't put the big monkey in jail.
The big monkey took my garbanzo bean and won't give it back.

STICK: Sorry, little monkey, but that's just too much trouble.

NARRATOR: So the little monkey went along and went along until she met a candle.

LITTLE MONKEY: Candle, burn the stick.
The stick won't scratch the cat.
The cat won't catch the rat.
The rat won't eat the king's robe.
The king won't put the big monkey in jail.
The big monkey took my garbanzo bean and won't give it back.

CANDLE: I'm too busy, little monkey. Come back later.

NARRATOR: So the little monkey went along and went along until she met some water.

LITTLE MONKEY: Water, put out the candle.
The candle won't burn the stick.
The stick won't scratch the cat.
The cat won't catch the rat.
The rat won't eat the king's robe.
The king won't put the big monkey in jail.
The big monkey took my garbanzo bean and won't give it back.

WATER: No, little monkey. The candle's smoke might get me dirty.

NARRATOR: So the little monkey went along and went along until she met a dog.

LITTLE MONKEY: Dog, drink the water.
The water won't put out the candle.
The candle won't burn the stick.

179

> The stick won't scratch the cat.
> The cat won't catch the rat.
> The rat won't eat the king's robe.
> The king won't put the big monkey in jail.
> The big monkey took my garbanzo bean and won't give it back.

Dog: Sorry, little monkey, I'm not thirsty right now.

Narrator: So the little monkey went along and went along until she met an ant.

Little Monkey: Ant, bite that dog.
> The dog won't drink the water.
> The water won't put out the candle.
> The candle won't burn the stick.
> The stick won't scratch the cat.
> The cat won't catch the rat.
> The rat won't eat the king's robe.
> The king won't put the big monkey in jail.
> The big monkey took my garbanzo bean and won't give it back.

Ant: What will you give me if I do?

Little Monkey: I'll share the garbanzo bean with you.

Ant: So I began to bite the dog.

Dog: Yow! And I began to drink the water.

Water: Stop that! And I began to put out the candle.

Candle: Fizzle, fizzle, fizzle. And I began to burn the stick.

Stick: Crackle, crackle, crackle. And I began to scratch the cat.

Cat: Meow! And I began to catch the rat.

Rat: Eek! And I began to eat the king's robe.

King: Get away, rat! And I began to put the big monkey in jail.

Big Monkey: Stop! Wait! Here, little monkey, take your garbanzo bean.

Little Monkey: It's about time! Little ant, do you want to eat the garbanzo bean now or plant it in the ground for later?

Ant: Let's plant it, and that way we'll have more next year.

Everyone: And they did.

BIBLIOGRAPHY

The folktales in this book do not come from one single source, but rather are blends of closely related folktale variants from one cultural area. I always work from as many sources as possible, some of which reside in my memory, recombining them to make an interesting tale for modern audiences in my part of the world. The one exception is "The Little Rabbit Who Wanted Red Wings," which appears in Carolyn Sherwin Bailey's *For the Storyteller*.

Aarne, Antti, and Stith Thompson. *The Types of the Folktale: A Classification and Bibliography.* 2d ed. Folklore Fellows Communications 184. Helsinki: Suomalainen Tiedeakatemia, 1961.

Baer, Florence E. *Sources and Analogues of the Uncle Remus Tales.* Folklore Fellows Communications 228. Helsinki: Suomalainen Tiedeakatemia, 1980.

Bailey, Carolyn Sherwin. *For the Storyteller.* Springfield, MA: Milton Bradley, 1920.

Barbeau, C. Marius, and Victor Morin. "Contes populaires canadiens." *Journal of American Folklore* 32 (1919).

Bascom, William. *African Dilemma Tales.* The Hague: Mouton, 1975.

———. *African Folktales in the New World.* Bloomington: Indiana University Press, 1992.

Baughman, Ernest Warren. *Type and Motif-Index of the Folktales of England and North America.* Indiana University Folklore Series, no. 20. The Hague: Mouton, 1966.

Bodker, Laurits. *Indian Animal Tales.* Folklore Fellows Communications 148. Helsinki: Suomalainen Tiedeakatemia, 1957.

Boggs, Ralph S. *Index of Spanish Folktales.* Folklore Fellows Communications 90. Helsinki: Suomalainen Tiedeakatemia, 1930.

Chambers, Robert. *Popular Rhymes of Scotland.* London: W. & R. Chambers, 1870.

Clarkson, Atelia, and Gilbert B. Cross. *World Folktales: A Treasury of Over Sixty of the World's Best-Loved Folktales.* New York: Scribner's, 1980.

Cole, Mabel Cook. *Philippine Folk Tales.* Chicago: A.C. McClurg & Co., 1916.

Delarue, Paul, and Marie-Louise Tenèze. *Le conte populaire français.* 4 vols. Paris: Érasme, 1957–1985.

Dixon, Roland B. *Mythology of All Races.* Vol. 9, Oceanic. Boston: Marshall Jones Co., 1916.

Dorson, Richard M. *Folktales Told around the World.* Chicago: University of Chicago Press, 1975.

Eastman, Mary Huse. *Index to Fairy Tales, Myths and Legends.* 2d ed. Boston: F. W. Faxon, 1926.

———. *Index to Fairy Tales, Myths and Legends.* Supplement. Boston: F. W. Faxon, 1937.

———. *Index to Fairy Tales, Myths and Legends.* 2nd Supplement. Boston: F. W. Faxon, 1952.

Eberhard, Wolfram. *Folktales of China.* Chicago: University of Chicago Press, 1965.

Espinosa, Aurelio M. *Cuentos Populares Españoles.* Stanford: Stanford University Press, 1923.

Fansler, Dean. *Filipino Popular Tales.* Hatboro, PA: Folklore Associates, 1965.

Feijoo, Samuel. *Cuentos Populares Cubanos.* Santa Clara, Cuba: Departamento de investigaciones folkloricas, Universidad Central de Las Villas, 1960–1962.

Fowke, Edith. *Folklore of Canada.* Toronto: McClelland & Stewart, 1976.

Griffis, William Elliot. *Korean Fairy Tales.* London: George G. Harrap, 1920.

Hansen, Terrence Leslie. *The Types of the Folktales in Cuba, Puerto Rico, the Dominican Republic and Spanish South America.* University of California Folklore Studies, No. 8. Berkeley: University of California Press, 1957.

Harris, Joel Chandler. *Uncle Remus and His Friends.* New York: Houghton Mifflin, 1892.

Im, Bang. *Korean Folktales.* London: J. M. Dent, 1913.

Jacobs, Joseph. *Celtic Fairy Tales.* London: David Nutt, 1892.

Jessup, Marie Hendrick, and Lesley Bird Simpson. *Indian Tales from Guatemala.* New York: Scribner's, 1936.

Jessup North Pacific Expedition. *The Eskimo of Siberia.* Vol. 8. Leiden: Jessup North Pacific Expedition, 1913.

Judson, Clara. *Myths and Legends of Alaska.* Chicago: A. C. McClurg, 1911.

Landes, Antony. *Contes et legendes annamites.* Saigon: Imprimerie Coloniale, 1886.

MacDonald, Margaret Read. *Storyteller's Sourcebook.* Detroit: Neal Schuman/Gale Research, 1982.

———. *Twenty Tellable Tales: Audience Participation Folktales for the Beginning Storyteller.* Bronx, NY: H. W. Wilson, 1986.

Parker, Henry. *Village Folk-Tales of Ceylon*. London: Luzoc & Co., 1910, 1914.

Rael, Juan B. *Cuentos Espanoles de Colorado y Nuevo Mejico* [sic]. Stanford: Stanford University Press, 1957.

Robe, Stanley L. *Hispanic Folktales from New Mexico*. Berkeley: University of California Press, 1977.

———. *Index of Mexican Folktales, Including Narrative Texts from Mexico, Central America and the Hispanic United States*. University of California Folklore Studies, No. 26. Berkeley: University of California Press, 1973.

Roberts, Warren. *South from Hell-fer-Sartin*. University of Kentucky Press, 1955.

Sierra, Judy, and Robert Kaminski. *Multicultural Folktales: Stories to Tell Young Children*. Phoenix, AZ: Oryx Press, 1991.

Skeat, Walter William. *Fables and Folk-Tales from an Eastern Forest*. Cambridge: Cambridge University Press, 1901.

Thompson, Stith. *Motif-Index of Folk-Literature*. 6 vols. Bloomington: Indiana Unviersity Press, 1955–1958.

Thompson, Stith, and Warren E. Roberts. *Types of Indic Oral Tales: India, Pakistan and Ceylon*. Folklore Fellows Communications 180. Helsinki: Suomalainen Tiedeakatemia, 1960.

Ting, Nai-Tung. *A Type Index of Chinese Folktales in the Oral Tradition and Major Works of Non-Religious Classical Literature*. Folklore Fellows Communications 223. Helsinki: Suomalainen Tiedeakatemia, 1978.

INDEX

by Linda Webster

African American folktale,
123–29
African dilemma tale, 62–67
Anglo-American folktales,
130–37, 146–53

"Bad Bear, The"
    feltboard storytelling,
        132
    patterns for feltboard
        figures, 133–34
    readers' theater play, 8,
        135–37
    text of story, 130–31
Bauer, Caroline, 9
"Bird and Her Babies, The"
    feltboard storytelling, 55
    patterns for feltboard
        figures, 56–59
    readers' theater play, 60–
        61
    text of story, 54–55
"Brer Rabbit's Riding Horse"
    feltboard storytelling,
        125

patterns for feltboard
    figures, 126–27
readers' theater play,
    128–29
text of story, 123–24

Canadian folktale, 154–62
Chinese folktale, 13–23
Cuban folktale, 171–80

"Eat, Coat, Eat!"
    feltboard storytelling,
        69–70
    patterns for feltboard
        figures, 71–73
    readers' theater play, 74–
        75
    text of story, 68–69

Feltboard figures
    making, 5–6
    for readers' theater, 10
Feltboard storytelling
    benefits of, 3

children as feltboard
    storytellers, 7–8
guidelines for, 3–4
making feltboard, 4
making feltboard figures,
    5–6
patterns in book for, 4–5
props and scenery for, 6
rehearsal for, 6–7
telling feltboard stories,
    7
Filipino folktale, 47–53
French-Canadian folktale,
    154–62

Guatemalan folktale, 163–70

Hispanic folktale, 138–45

Indonesian folktale, 30–37
Inuit folktale, 116–22
Irish folktale, 85–96

"Juan and the Ghost"
feltboard storytelling, 139–40
patterns for feltboard figures, 141–43
readers' theater play, 144–45
text of story, 138–39

"Kanchil and the Crocodile"
feltboard storytelling, 32
patterns for feltboard figures, 33–34
readers' theater play, 35–37
text of story, 30–32
Korean folktale, 38–46
Koryak folktale, 107–15

"Little Ant, The"
feltboard storytelling, 78
patterns for feltboard figures, 79–82
readers' theater play, 83–84
text of story, 76–77

"Mouse and the Coal, The"
feltboard storytelling, 156
patterns for feltboard figures, 157–59
readers' theater play, 160–62
text of story, 154–56
"Munachar and Manachar"
feltboard storytelling, 88
patterns for feltboard figures, 89–92
readers' theater play, 93–96
text of story, 85–88

New Mexican folktale, 138–45
"New Year's Animals, The"
feltboard storytelling, 14–15
patterns for feltboard figures, 16–21
readers' theater play, 22–23
text of story, 13–14

Patterns for feltboards, 4–5
Presenting Readers' Theater (Bauer), 9
Props for feltboards, 6

"Rabbit and the Tiger, The"
feltboard storytelling, 25–26
patterns for feltboard figures, 27
readers' theater play, 28–29
text of story, 24–25
"Rabbit Who Wanted Red Wings, The"
feltboard storytelling, 147–48
patterns for feltboard figures, 149–50
readers' theater play, 151–53
text of story, 146–47
Readers' theater, 8–10
Rehearsal for feltboard storytelling, 6–7
Rod puppets, 10

Scenery for feltboards, 6
Scottish folktale, 97–106
Siberian folktale, 107–15
Spanish folktale, 76–84
Sri Lankan folktale, 54–61
"Strongest of All"
feltboard storytelling, 40
patterns for feltboard figures, 41–43
readers' theater play, 44–46
text of story, 38–40

"Talkative Tortoise, The"
feltboard storytelling, 165
patterns for feltboard figures, 166–67
readers' theater play, 168–70
text of story, 163–64
"Through the Needle's Eye"
feltboard storytelling, 117–18

patterns for feltboard figures, 119–20
readers' theater play, 121–22
text of story, 116–17
"Tricks of a Fox, The"
feltboard storytelling, 108–09
patterns for feltboard figures, 110–13
readers' theater play, 114–15
text of story, 107–08
Turkish folktale, 68–75
"Two Monkeys, The"
feltboard storytelling, 174
patterns for feltboard figures, 175–77
readers' theater play, 8, 178–80
text of story, 171–73

Vietnamese folktale, 24–29

"Water Buffalo and the Snail, The"
feltboard storytelling, 49
patterns for feltboard figures, 50–51
readers' theater play, 52–53
text of story, 47–48
"Wee Bannock, The"
feltboard storytelling, 99
patterns for feltboard figures, 100–03
readers' theater play, 8, 104–06
text of story, 97–98
"Wolf, the Goat, and the Cabbages, The"
feltboard storytelling, 63
patterns for feltboard figures, 64–65
readers' theater play, 66–67
text of story, 62–63